ASTD Trainer's WorkShop Series

Manager Skills
TRAINING

Christee Gabour Atwood

ASTD Press is an internationally renowned source of insightful and practical information on workplace learning and performance topics, including training basics, evaluation and return-on-investment (ROI), instructional systems development (ISD), e-learning, leadership, and career development.

Ordering information: Books published by ASTD Press can be purchased by visiting our website at store.astd.org or by calling 800.628.2783 or 703.683.8100.

Library of Congress Control Number: 2007939862

ISBN-10: 1-56286-516-1
ISBN-13: 978-1-56286-516-0

ASTD Press Editorial Staff:
Director: Cat Russo
Manager, Acquisitions and Author Relations: Mark Morrow
Editorial Manager: Jacqueline Edlund-Braun
Editorial Assistant: Maureen Soyars
Copyeditor: Pamela Lankas
Indexer: Mary Kidd
Proofreader: IGS
Interior Design and Production: International Graphic Services
Cover Design: Steve Fife
Cover Illustrator: Todd Davidson

Printed by Victor Graphics, Inc., Baltimore, Maryland, www.victorgraphics.com

The ASTD Trainer's WorkShop Series

◆

The ASTD Trainer's WorkShop Series is designed to be a practical, hands-on road map to help you quickly develop training in key business areas. Each book in the series offers all the exercises, handouts, assessments, structured experiences, and ready-to-use presentations needed to develop effective training sessions. In addition to easy-to-use icons, each book in the series includes a companion CD-ROM or website with PowerPoint presentations and electronic copies of all supporting material featured in the book.

Other books in the Trainer's WorkShop Series:

- ◆ ***New Supervisor Training***
  John E. Jones and Chris W. Chen

- ◆ ***New Employee Orientation Training***
  Karen Lawson

- ◆ ***Leading Change Training***
  Jeffrey Russell and Linda Russell

- ◆ ***Leadership Training***
  Lou Russell

- ◆ ***Coaching Training***
  Chris W. Chen

- ◆ ***Project Management Training***
  Bill Shackelford

Contents

When someone asks you about the best manager you ever knew, usually a specific person comes to mind.

That manager might have had outstanding communication skills, speaking *with* us and not *at* us. He or she probably knew not to use a "two-dollar word" when a "25-cent word" would serve the same purpose. That manager was usually one who knew that tone and body language play a bigger role in conversations than words do. Even more important, he or she probably understood that the most important communication skill is listening, not speaking.

Perhaps that manager had empathy and was truly able to stand in another's shoes.

That manager was decisive and, once the decision was made, was willing to stick behind the choice and behind the team without wavering. That manager was probably the special kind of person who gave credit and took blame.

He or she had true enthusiasm, the desire to help others succeed, and an understanding of the big picture, which included the idea that success is best when it is shared. Certainly that manager was observant and able to recognize and address challenges before they weakened the workplace. And always, that manager was the type whom we would have followed even if he or she did not have the title.

I'm lucky. I've dealt with hundreds of managers who fit this definition. No, I haven't had that many jobs. Well, not quite that many. But in my workshops I've had the opportunity to meet hundreds of the best kinds of managers. They were special because they knew that none of us should ever stop learning. They weren't just managers. They were leaders.

No matter how accomplished we are or how successful we become, the desire to keep learning and to continue developing our skills is what sets a true leader apart from other managers. The sessions in this book give participants opportunities to practice the skills of effective management and leadership. These workshops also take into consideration that, when you have a room full of individuals, each brings different talents and insights. The exercises are designed to allow participants to share those insights, because many of the best lessons learned in any workshop are those gathered from fellow learners. Of course, this is tough for us facilitators who would like to think that we're the smartest ones in the room . . .

And so, this book is dedicated to those managers I have learned so much from, and to the participants still to come who help me to keep learning.

Christee Gabour Atwood
Louisiana, USA
2008

Introduction: How to Use This Book Effectively

What's in This Chapter

- Discussion of the benefits of manager skills training
- Explanation of how to use this book for best results
- Description of what's in this workbook and on the accompanying website

The wonderful words, "Congratulations, you've been promoted!" can also be the downfall of many dedicated employees.

We've gone to school, studied, and worked hard to learn to efficiently perform the skills needed for our positions. But, until recent years, there has been no focus on helping us develop the specific skills that are needed to become a successful manager. We just assumed that, if a person was a good accountant, that person would also be a good manager of accountants.

The challenge is that the skills needed to be a good accountant are not the same set of skills necessary to be an effective manager. As a result, many excellent employees have been promoted without preparation for their new roles, have been unable to adapt, and thus have been lost. Then, the company has not only lost a manager, but a valuable employee.

How can this workshop help?

By taking the time to prepare our managers for the different skill sets that are required of their positions, we can help situate them for success. And, if they receive training in advance of the promotion, they can discover whether they possess the needed competencies before they are put into the position to "sink or swim."

This is also the time when we can reinforce the concept that all movement within the company doesn't necessarily have to be upward to be rewarding. If, on reviewing these skills, employees discover that they're not comfortable with the responsibilities that are expected of managers, they can adjust their career plans to grow in the organization through expanded responsibilities or lateral moves to other areas of specialization.

Who needs this course?

Managers at all levels and at any point in their careers can use this workshop as either an orientation or as a refresher course. An important trait of the effective manager is the willingness to be a constant learner, and one's participation in this course demonstrates that trait. Additionally, the course will update the manager on the latest trends in management development.

How can this workbook help?

In this workbook, you'll study the core concepts of management and methods to help you apply those concepts effectively. The goal of this book is to give you a "class in a box," so you can step in and present anything from a one-hour overview to a two-day workshop to your audience. And, by choosing the segments that are most appropriate for your group, you can tailor the workshop to your specific needs.

This book can help your organization's members prepare themselves effectively for manager roles. It will help current managers assess their skills and create an action plan for continued development.

How to Use This Workbook

Whether you're an experienced facilitator or a novice instructor, you'll find that this workbook is a useful resource for developing and facilitating workshops on manager skills and, by substituting exercises or segments, you'll be able to customize the programs to meet the specific needs of your audiences.

The training materials in this book and on the accompanying website (www.ASTD.org/ManagerSkillsTraining) include

- ◆ Tools and strategies for assessing manager skills and needs.

- ◆ Guidelines for designing your manager skills workshops.

- ◆ Materials and instructions for facilitating your training sessions.

◆ Strategies and tools for evaluating the workshops.

◆ Training workshop formats and agendas that incorporate a range of training activities. The agendas can be used "as is" or modified to suit your organization's needs and your facilitation style.

◆ Learning activities, tools, and assessments designed to support the workshops.

◆ Microsoft PowerPoint presentations accompany each workshop format. You'll find thumbnails of the slides at the ends of the chapters in which they are used. The website also contains black-and-white versions of the slides that can be printed three-to-a-page and used as class handouts.

All of the assessments, instruments, and tools can be found on the website. Prepare these in advance by copying them on hole-punched paper. Then insert the PowerPoint handouts into the three-ring binders for your attendees. You'll distribute the rest of the handouts and tools at appropriate times during the workshop.

Here are some suggestions for using this book effectively:

◆ **Skim the book.** Browse the table of contents of this workbook. Study the "What's in This Chapter?" lists. Get an overall sense of the layout and structure of the information that's included.

◆ **Be sure you understand the basics of effective management skills.** Spend some time studying the overview of manager skills by reviewing chapter 2 and by consulting some of the resources listed in the Resources section at the end of this workbook. Find opportunities to identify and learn from outstanding managers in your company and find mentors in your business community to interview for additional insights.

◆ **Assess the needs for manager skills in your organization.** Take the time to consider the benefits of manager skills training and how this could help your organization. For example, imagine how productivity could be increased if every manager practiced time management and project management techniques. Consider how employee satisfaction could be increased if managers improved their communication skills. Using information from chapter 3, consider the current manager skill levels and decide where the greatest need for improved performance exists. Then use the ideas in chapter 4 to design a workshop specifically focused on that need.

◆ **Review the methods for presenting a high-impact program.** Chapter 5 outlines ideas for making your program successful. You'll learn techniques for helping attendees become more comfortable as they participate in the activities and practice sessions during the course of the workshop. You'll incorporate the core concepts that you're sharing with attendees so that you are setting the example for them—modeling the coaching and communication behaviors you want them to develop.

◆ **Study the sample program agendas.** By reviewing the agendas for the one-hour, half-day, one-day, and two-day formats, you can decide which format will address and satisfy your group's specific needs. Go through each agenda, even if you don't plan to present all the workshop formats. You may discover an exercise in one agenda that isn't included in the format you plan to use but that would be a great benefit to your specific participants. Simply replace an exercise in the agenda you're using with one from the other programs. The time listings on each activity will help you make replacements and adjust the schedule to fit your desired workshop length.

◆ **Design *your* training program.** Because this workbook includes everything you need for a workshop, you can use your time to make the program your own instead of spending time creating agendas and formulating exercises. You can mold the workshop and incorporate your own personality into it to make the presentation suit your style. When the program fits you, you'll get more pleasure from presenting it and you'll be more effective in communicating the concepts to your learners.

What's on the Website?

All of the assessments, tools, training instruments, and PowerPoint slides used in this workbook are included on the accompanying website (www.ASTD.org/ManagerSkillsTraining) so you can easily run the PowerPoint presentations and print out copies of the learning materials. Follow the instructions in the Appendix, "Using the Website," at the back of the workbook.

Icons

For easy reference and to help you quickly locate specific materials and tools for training design and instructions, icons are included in the margins throughout this workbook. Here are the icons and what they represent:

Assessment: Appears when an agenda or learning activity includes an assessment.

Website: Indicates materials included on the website accompanying this workbook.

DOWNLOADS

Clock: Indicates suggested timeframes for an activity.

Key Point: Alerts you to pivotal concepts that you should emphasize to the participants or that are particularly salient for you as the facilitator.

Learning Activity: Indicates a structured exercise for use in a training session.

PowerPoint Item: Indicates PowerPoint presentations and individual slides.

Tool: Identifies an item offering information that participants will find useful in the training session and on the job.

Training Instrument: Indicates interactive training materials for participant use.

What to Do Next: Denotes recommendations for what to do after completing a particular section of the workbook.

What to Do Next

- Study the contents of the workbook to familiarize yourself with the material it offers.

- Complete the assessments in the workbook to rate your own coaching, communication, and other manager skills, and to determine areas that you need to develop.

- Review the contents of the website and open some of the items so you understand how the materials are organized and accessed.

◆ ◆ ◆

The next chapter identifies the basics required to facilitate a manager skills workshop effectively. You'll be introduced to some of the terminology, concepts, and steps to creating a high-impact workshop that will help your attendees not only learn the needed skills, but also enjoy the experience.

Key Concepts of Manager Skills

- ◆ Terms and concepts of effective manager skills
- ◆ Section-by-section overview of comprehensive manager skills training

The key concepts addressed in this workbook are of real-world value for your workshop participants, and they're excellent reminders to you as a communicator and coach. What follows is an overview of the key aspects of the management topics that are covered in the various workshop activities.

Workshop Formats

This workbook offers four workshop agendas, based on the amount of time available for training. The two-day workshop is the complete manager skills course, offering all topics for a comprehensive manager skills training course. The other three formats are condensed versions, offering either shorter versions of the activities or concentrating on basic manager skills and deleting the nonessential topics.

The following overview outlines the full two-day workshop format to explain the flow of topics and activities. If you find that you'll be offering a shorter-format workshop, this outline will give you an idea of all the segments available, so you can select those that will be most relevant for your organization.

The two-day workshop focuses equally on the two main skill areas in which effective managers excel. These skill areas are often referred to as *hard* and *soft* competencies. Hard, or functional competencies, are those skills that deal with the technical and process-related aspects of their positions. The soft skills are those competencies that deal with behavioral or human resource issues, often referred to as interpersonal or people skills.

The first section of the workshop allows your learners to assess themselves to determine what areas they are proficient in and which skills require further development. You'll probably find a range of experience in your session participants—from new managers-in-training to seasoned managers, who might be reluctant to participate in workshop.

With careful facilitation of your workshop and continual solicitation of best practices from your experienced managers, it's possible to see even those seasoned managers move toward active involvement in the session.

The basic manager skills that are addressed in this workshop are listed by topic. Day One focuses on the people or *soft* skills that a manager needs to interact effectively with his or her team, supervisors, other departments, and the general public. An assessment will help learners identify areas that need development. The segments of this workshop are designed to introduce the subjects and then allow the participants to make additional discoveries during the course of the activities that follow.

- Interpersonal Skills—This section addresses both listening and communication skills, as well as a segment on observation skills, which allow learners to focus on interpreting the cues that their employees are sending.

- Coaching—The ability to recognize the need for coaching, the steps of an effective coaching session, and individual breakouts to practice using those steps are included in this section of the course.

- Motivating Employees—This segment discusses the main motivators for employees and then allows teams to create reward and recognition programs to respond to those motivators.

- Resolving Conflict—In this section, participants will learn the difference between good and bad conflict in the workplace. They'll receive tools and information to help in the resolution of conflicts and have an opportunity to practice using those tools to address samples of typical workplace scenarios.

- Presentation Skills—The ability to effectively present themselves in varying formats to different audiences is a vital skill that is addressed in this section. Participants will practice condensing their messages to be as brief as possible as they create elevator speeches.

- Facilitation Skills—Surveys have revealed that much of the time spent in meetings is considered wasted time. To combat this statistic, participants will learn the steps they can take before, during, and after meetings to ensure that their meetings are an asset, not a liability.

- Encouraging Creativity and Innovation—Participants will review the rules and tools of brainstorming to encourage input and ideas from their employees.

- Customer Service—To lead by example, managers need to exhibit outstanding customer service skills. In this section of the workshop, customer-service formulas will be studied and then practiced with customer-challenge situations.

- Written Communications—The written documents produced by a manager must be professional, accurate, and positive. This segment gives basic guidelines for effective documents and allows participants to practice by creating a sample email or memo.

The focus of Day Two is on functional or *hard* skills. These skills deal with the tasks, the processes, and the procedures of making the work happen. The discussion and practice time of any of these topics can be expanded to suit your organization's needs by eliminating other subjects that are not applicable to your group.

- Time Management—Participants will review the basics of effective time management, discuss common time wasters, and practice prioritizing and scheduling their time in this activity.

- Project Management—The fundamentals of project management will be reviewed in this segment, which allows the group to brainstorm the steps of a project and create an ordered plan with deadlines, resources, and assignments.

- Decision Making—In this segment, participants will receive a number of valuable tools to assist them in making decisions individually or as part of a group planning session. An exercise will allow them to practice using these tools with a group.

- Records Management—This section includes guidelines used to organize files, employee records, financials, and other essential documentation that managers need on a regular basis.

- Performance Management—The three phases of performance management are explained in this section. This section culminates with a practice session of a performance appraisal that allows learners to perform the steps of an appraisal session and receive coaching and input from fellow attendees.

◆ Creating Teams—Participants will discuss the diverse personalities that either make teams effective or block progress, depending on how they are handled. They'll practice by creating solutions for common team challenges.

◆ Problem Solving—This section offers a practical application of the information from the session on actual issues that are current problems for managers. Attendees will trade problems with others for a problem-solving session and will be able to leave with immediate ideas to address those challenges.

◆ Knowledge Management—In this overview, attendees will be introduced to the concepts of knowledge management, succession planning, and other current trends in education and development.

The workshop closes with the preparation of individual development plans for participants that will support the transfer and continued application of this new knowledge into their workplace practices.

What to Do Next

◆ Review the agenda of the two-day workshop to see which activities target the needs of your group.

◆ Determine the length of the workshop you'll offer.

◆ Tailor the content of the workshop to suit your organization's and participants' needs.

◆ Make room and equipment reservations.

◆ ◆ ◆

If you need help determining the requirements of your group, go to the next chapter, where we'll look more closely at the process of assessing your organization's needs and at the various instruments that can help you in that task.

Assessing Your Organization's Needs

- Discussion of employee needs assessments
- Overview of assessment procedures
- Reviewing assessment results

Overview of Assessment Procedures

The good news is that there's always room for growth in the skill areas that are discussed in this workshop, so any time that you present this program, participants will benefit from the discussion and activities. However, it is an advantage to study your organization as much as possible so that your programs address real needs and support the latest strategic plans and directions of the organization.

The basic tools for assessing your organization's needs include records and testing, interviews and surveys, and requests. The most effective needs assessment includes elements of all of these tools.

RECORDS AND TESTING

Records can be accumulated from as early as the hiring process and throughout the lifetime of employees, including skill assessments, individual development plans, competency listings for positions in your organization, and employee performance reviews based on those competencies. By compiling this information, you can begin to identify skill gaps that could be addressed by training.

INTERVIEWS AND SURVEYS

Interviews and surveys of employees and supervisors can help you discover where a lack of management skill might be hindering some employees' advancement in the organization. It's essential that any survey you conduct be confidential and free from bias so that you can get open, honest responses. Many survey formats are available, ranging from basic to comprehensive. Your best choice is the simplest survey that meets your needs. If the survey is too involved or time-consuming, your response rate will be low and you won't get a representative sample.

Additionally, interviews of senior management team members can be helpful in the planning of your programs. Understanding the direction of the organization, any impending changes or initiatives, and other related business plans can help you ensure that your program includes the skills to address those changes. For example, if the organization is planning to move to a paperless system, records management and technical skills might be more prominent in your workshops.

TRAINING REQUESTS

Requests submitted by employees or managers are good indicators of the need for training, but should be used in conjunction with a personal interview to ensure that you are addressing the actual needs and not just an issue that is a symptom of a bigger challenge. Taking the time to ask additional questions and discovering exactly what the desired outcome is after the employee completes the training may help you determine whether the request is truly a training issue, or if it's a behavioral problem or even a workplace process that needs revisiting.

The main point here is to apply the same investigation process you'd use to find out if an employee needs a coaching session to determine if training is the right answer to the request that you've received.

Analyzing Your Assessment Results

To identify where training needs are greatest, your best plan includes balancing input from a variety of these assessment sources. In that way you can make an informed decision on what training topics and development activities are most important to your organization at this time.

By studying the results of the surveys and interviews, you'll have a better understanding of which skills the employees are lacking. Then you can even customize your class by addressing specific areas with shorter-format workshops from this workbook—for example, you might find that mini-sessions concentrating on communication skills or performance management procedures are the best ways to address your group's needs.

What to Do Next

- ◆ Review any reports, training requests, surveys, interviews, and records that you have gathered.

- ◆ Compile and analyze the results to determine organizational or individual gaps in manager skills.

- ◆ Begin the communication process to identify candidates for the workshop among members of the organization.

◆ ◆ ◆

In chapter 4, you'll look at ways you can create customized workshops from the materials in this workbook. Doing so will allow you to focus a program on manager challenges that meet the immediate and long-term needs of your organization.

◆

Designing the Workshop

What's in This Chapter

- Instructions for defining your workshop goals
- Guidelines for preparing the learning environment
- Methods for communicating your workshop goals to the organization

While you are designing the workshop you have the opportunity to make the program unique to your organization and suit it to your particular training style. This is when your creative side gets to play. You'll be able to choose and adapt the exercises that are the best match for your organizational culture. You'll consider what classroom setting will be most effective, and you'll determine the tone of your communications about the workshop.

Determining Workshop Goals

Review the results of your organizational assessments and interviews to identify the workshop format and topics that are appropriate for your learners' needs.

You'll use this information to determine the objectives for your workshop. Workshop objectives are simply the behaviors and skills that you want your participants to be able to demonstrate after attending the session.

Each version of the workshop lists objectives. You can use these as listed if you present that workshop in its entirety. However, if you see an objective from one of the other versions that you want to add to your session, just insert that objective and its supporting activities. Then you'll need to adjust your time or remove other activities to make the length of the session fit your needs.

Perhaps your group is going to be composed completely of new managers. You'll want to give them as much information as time will allow. For experienced managers, you might focus on the practical application exercises, such as performance management and coaching skills.

Once you've identified the specific needs of your organization and the corresponding objectives for your workshop, take the time to communicate them clearly in all of your workshop promotion pieces.

Establishing a Learning Environment

Creating the right environment for a workshop is vital to hosting a successful event. Here are some basic concepts that you'll want to keep in mind.

A workshop is an interactive session that includes writing and small-group breakouts. The best seating arrangement for a group of 15 or more will be a chevron shape—basically, an angled classroom-style arrangement with tables forming a V. Learners will use the tables for note taking, and the angled arrangement lets participants see each other and interact. Leave an alley down the center and enough space between the tables so you can walk around and monitor progress during the learning activities.

If space doesn't allow the use of chevron-style seating, opt for classroom seating, which simply consists of rows of tables and chairs. You wouldn't want to use theater seating (rows of chairs without tables) for this session because of the amount of writing they'll be doing.

If your group is smaller than 15 attendees, a U-shape layout is an excellent option. This allows maximum interaction among the participants and allows you to move to any learner easily.

Any of these setups can work for your session. Just remember that your main considerations are: (1) learners need tables for writing, and (2) they need enough room so that they will be able to break out into smaller groups for the activities and practice sessions.

Use the checklists included in the course materials to ensure you have all the materials you need and to design a training environment that encourages interaction.

This workshop offers an opportunity to use all those facilitator tools that make a session effective. Collect table toys so that the kinesthetic learners have something to occupy their hands. These might include peg games, stress balls, and other assorted dexterity puzzles. Put up posters and incorporate color into the room for your visual learners' enjoyment. And have music playing when participants enter and during the learning activities for your auditory learners.

Getting the Word Out

Communicating the goals of your workshop to the organization and prospective attendees is vital, not only to ensure attendance, but also to be sure that attendees know what to expect when they get to the workshop.

The manager skills workshop you're preparing to conduct is interactive and enjoyable, so let that fact show in your communications. As you send out information about the workshop, clearly state the goals and what participants can expect in the session using positive, active language. Remind them of these goals whenever you contact them by email. It's discouraging to everyone involved when a person has an unrealistic idea of what will be covered in a workshop. Don't put anyone in that situation.

Watch for other opportunities to promote the workshop, such as newsletters, bulletin boards, staff meetings, and management sessions. Many businesses even use their elevators as space to promote upcoming training.

And don't underestimate the power of awarding certificates to graduates. Receiving a certificate reinforces feelings of accomplishment and creates pride in those who've participated. They'll probably hang the certificates in their cubicles, and a certificate on the wall is seen much more often than a flyer from the training department.

What to Do Next

- ◆ Finalize your goals for the program.

- ◆ Visit the room where you'll be holding the program to determine the layout you will use for your classroom and how many attendees it will accommodate.

- ◆ Create a promotional plan for your workshop, thinking of new places and ways to get the word out.

- ◆ Design and distribute flyers, emails, and information on the program.

- ◆ Prepare your checklist and timeline.

◆ ◆ ◆

In the first part of this workbook you've been assessing, planning, and coordinating the logistics of your program. In the next chapter you'll change hats and start to prepare for the program as a facilitator.

◆

Facilitating the Workshop

What's in This Chapter

- ◆ Overview of workshop preparations
- ◆ Instructions for preparing participant materials
- ◆ Explanation of the principles of effective facilitation

The term *facilitation* signifies the point at which we go beyond the concept of lecturing into interactive and experiential learning. We all know that learners remember 10 percent of what they hear; 20 percent of what they see; 65 percent of what they hear and see; and 90 percent of what they *hear, see,* and *do*. This is the principle that drives the activities in your management skills workshop. Your learners will be "doing" a lot in the sessions to ensure maximum retention of the skills they learn and practice there.

Workshop Preparations

It's best if you can set up your room the day before the session begins. This enables you to deal with any problems caused by missing or faulty equipment and ensures that you're not sweaty and worn out from moving tables and equipment at 8:00 a.m. when your attendees arrive.

Set your facilitator table with your instructor's guide and all the hole-punched handouts that you'll give out to the attendees at different points during the workshop. Load your CD player with suitable music and turn on your computer with the Microsoft PowerPoint presentation loaded directly onto the hard drive.

Also, have a supply of basic items for your own convenience, including a glass of water, mints, headache remedies, and tissues. Outfit yourself with whatever other items you think you'll need.

Check the markers and flipcharts. You don't want to find you have a dry marker or only two sheets of paper. You'll also want to have dry-erase markers (and know which ones are which), masking tape torn into strips and attached to the back of the flipchart easel so you can quickly post pages around the room, and a timer to keep up with the exercises. A prize bag is an optional item that's always a big hit. Just load it up with rewards from your local dollar store, which can be a fun incentive to get attendees into the spirit of competition.

If there's a phone in the room, check to see what you have to do to silence it for the duration of the workshop. Find out how to operate the thermostat. Learn where the light switches are. And ask about fire exits and restroom locations if you are in a building where you don't normally work.

Be sure the room is set for the appropriate number of attendees. Take a seat in the back row as well as around the outer edges of the tables to confirm that everyone will have a good view of the screen and of all activity at the front of the room.

When you feel confident that you've addressed all the details of your meeting room, prepare the site for your attendees.

Participant Materials

Set the following materials at each attendee's place:

- a binder filled with the handouts and extra paper for notes

- a few sticky-notes attached to the front of the binder

- pencils or pens

- a name badge (don't use table tents because your learners move around during the workshop).

Place the following materials on each table for group use:

- markers for activities that require flipcharting

- a few flipchart pages

- snacks, mints, and so forth

- toys or gadgets to keep restless hands busy but that don't distract from the learning activities.

Principles of Effective Facilitation

Once you've set the stage, you're ready to focus on facilitation techniques. Here are some of the best practices to help guarantee the success of your session:

- Set ground rules at the beginning of the session. These rules can include the procedure for breaks; respectful communication reminders, such as only one person speaking at a time, and that all cell phones should be silenced. Be sure to turn off your cell phone at the same time you tell them to silence theirs. That's another opportunity to lead by example.

- Use verbal and nonverbal reinforcement techniques to create rapport. Watch for nonverbal cues. Are they fidgeting? Do they look confused? Is anyone dozing off? Are people putting on sweaters? Respond as needed to the cues you receive.

- Use appropriate humor as a communication tool, but don't feel it's necessary to tell jokes. Not all of us are meant to be stand-up comedians.

- Keep lecture time to a minimum. If you find that a segment of the workshop is not eliciting enough discussion, modify the format to let the participants teach that section. It's your workshop; you make the rules.

- Count to 10 after you ask a question. One of the big challenges for facilitators is to let a moment of silence pass. Just remember that the participants don't know this material like you do. It takes them a little longer to process the new information, make connections, and respond to your queries.

- Check frequently for understanding. Ask your learners if they understand the topic you're discussing. Have them summarize the main points of the material you presented.

- Handle aggressive behavior by remaining calm. Acknowledge and immediately move the focus to problem solving. You might even allow the group to help you deal with the problem, as long as you do this diplomatically and are careful not to demean the individuals involved.

- If problem behavior persists, take a break and privately discuss the situation with the disruptive participant. Remember, yours is the final word. You have the right to define the limits of acceptable behavior and to ask a person who is going beyond those limits to leave the workshop.

◆ Incorporate words that appeal to the different learning styles. For your visual learners, use phrases like, "Let's take a look at this." Auditory learners respond well to hearing-oriented phrases like, "How does that sound?" And your kinesthetic learners feel comfortable with phrases like, "How did that exercise feel to you?"

◆ During activities, it's a good idea to walk around and check on your participants. Some people will finish early and start other conversations. Others will struggle to get started. By continually moving among the groups, you can keep everyone focused on the task at hand and ensure they're doing the activity in the way it's intended. Ask questions such as: Did any other questions come up over here? What's the hardest thing about this exercise so far? Is this one working for you?

◆ At various intervals during the session, ask how this information could be useful to the learners in their departments. This reinforces the concept of taking this learning back into the workplace.

◆ If you see people who are staying quiet, try to include them in the discussion on a simple question or directly ask their opinion.

◆ Don't be surprised if you can't answer all your learners' questions. Ask for ideas from the group. Write down the questions you can't answer or have the questioner write it on a sticky-note and put it in a "parking lot" area on a flipchart page. Then you can get an answer after the class and distribute the answer to everyone. The good news here is that every question you have to get an answer for is a question you'll know the answer to next time around.

◆ In the sample agendas included in this workbook, there are estimates of the blocks of time each section will take. These times will give you a general idea of how far ahead or behind schedule you're running. If you see that you're falling too far behind, make adjustments by limiting discussion or asking participants to save their questions until the end of the segment. If you're moving too fast, maybe you're not allowing sufficient time for participants to talk. In that case, stop at the next opportunity and ask for questions on what has been discussed thus far.

◆ If you're running out of time in a class, look through the upcoming exercises and choose ones that you can cover in discussions instead of using the scheduled exercises.

◆ Make notes of the actual timing of the workshop and write these in the margins of your manual during the class so you can adjust your agenda planning for future workshop presentations.

◆ You can give your learners data. You can show them charts. You can have them read the handouts and complete the exercises. But the best learning that will occur in that room comes from the example that you set with your behavior, your enthusiasm, and your sincere desire to share the information with them. Set the example by being a highly motivated professional.

What to Do Next

◆ Review the checklist that accompanies the workshop version you have chosen and determine the materials needed and what is required to complete your workshop plans.

◆ Prepare the handouts and purchase all supplies.

◆ Monitor registration and send confirmation emails.

◆ Check the room setup and make sure all equipment is working properly.

◆ ◆ ◆

The next chapter will help you evaluate the effectiveness of your workshops so you can continue to develop and adjust the sessions to meet the needs of your organization.

◆

Evaluating the Workshop

What's in This Chapter

- ◆ Discussion of the benefits of workshop evaluations
- ◆ Information on expanded evaluation methods
- ◆ Review of the criteria to be evaluated

Evaluations, a valuable tool for improving our skills, are often overlooked. In many cases, evaluations are distributed in the last minutes of a session when participants are anxious to leave and unwilling to spend time giving meaningful comments.

In the same way that a current customer is our best tool for enhancing company performance, a participant who has just completed our program is the best barometer of the program's effectiveness.

Additionally, a presenter's willingness to be evaluated by the attendees sends an important message. If that facilitator is committed to continual improvement, it reminds the participants that they, too, need to be willing to continue developing their abilities.

Expanded Evaluation Methods

Most evaluations include a 1-to-5 scale for rating class content, environment, and facilitation. Such a simple rating often is all that participants will have the time to complete. But adding a few additional questions to your survey and making certain you provide enough time for your learners to give you thoughtful answers can yield a wealth of information.

Here are several sample questions to include

- ◆ What did you learn from this workshop that you'll be able to use in your job?

- What would you like to see more of in this workshop?

- What would you like to see less of in this workshop?

If you allow five extra minutes for attendees to complete evaluations, including these questions, you can harvest a great many honest perceptions of the value of your workshops and of your presentation style.

Here are some other ideas for making the most effective use of your evaluation forms.

- Turn your evaluation form into a preassessment and a postassessment form. For the preassessment portion, include these questions:

  1. What is something you already know about manager skills?

  2. What area of manager skills would you like to learn more about?

  3. How would you rate your management skill level?

- For the postassessment portion, include these questions:

  1. What is something you learned today about manager skills?

  2. Did you learn anything about the area you cited in preassessment question 2?

  3. How would you rate your manager skills after this class?

- Evaluation through class discussion also can be useful if prefaced correctly. It's important to let the participants know that their comments are being accepted in the spirit of development and that you will not be offended by anything they say.

- Send a 30-day follow-up letter, asking if managers are using the information and techniques they practiced in the workshop. This offers you an opportunity to receive additional evaluations of your program. You might also adapt the letter and send it to the attendee's supervisor to ask if he or she has noticed any change in the manager's communication, coaching, or project management skills. Use the letter to invite attendees to a follow-up session to see what skills the person has developed as a result of the workshop. This letter is also a chance to gather dathat defines your training initiative's return-on-investment—something that the organization's managers will be interested in knowing and consequentially will help you justify more resources for your program.

◆ Informal evaluations or interviews are also useful information-gathering tools. Simply visiting with those who have completed the class can give you ideas about which material worked and what revisions need to be made for the next presentation.

Criteria to Be Evaluated

Here are samples of the basic criteria you'll want to evaluate for any workshops you present. These criteria can be included in survey forms, evaluations, follow-up studies, or classroom discussions:

◆ Participants enjoyed the program.

◆ Participants received the information they needed or wanted.

◆ Activities and methods responsive to the principles of adult learning were built into the course.

◆ The course appealed to visual, auditory, and kinesthetic learners.

◆ Content was relevant to participants' jobs.

◆ Participants had the opportunity to practice the new skills being taught.

◆ Time spent on practice and feedback was adequate.

◆ Course materials were designed to be used as on-the-job aids.

◆ Learners were motivated to use the new skills back on the job.

◆ Facilitator was effective in communicating the materials.

What to Do Next

◆ Review the agenda for the workshop you'll be presenting.

◆ Create all handouts and tools from the materials on the accompanying website.

◆ Determine what formats you'll implement for evaluation and follow-up.

◆ ◆ ◆

The next chapters present step-by-step agendas and instructions for each of the workshop formats.

Chapter 7

One-Hour Program

- Objectives for the one-hour manager skills workshop
- Lists of materials for facilitator and participants
- Detailed program agenda to be used as a facilitator's guide

The one-hour workshop teaches learners the concepts of interpersonal and functional manager skills. It also introduces the concepts of knowledge management. The one-hour workshop is an overview session, without in-depth analysis.

Training Objectives

The participants' objectives for the one-hour manager skills workshop are to be able to

- explain the differences between interpersonal and functional manager skills
- demonstrate a basic understanding of knowledge management
- begin a plan for development of manager skills.

Materials

For the facilitator:

- this chapter for reference and use as a facilitator guide
- Assessment 12–2: Evaluation Form
- Training Instrument 12–17: Development Plan

- Tool 12–16: Performance Management Process

- Tool 12–19: Knowledge Management

- Tool 12–20: Individual Development Plan

- PowerPoint slide program, entitled "Manager Skills" (slides 7–1 through 7–15). To access slides for this program, open the file *One hour.ppt* on the website. Thumbnail versions of the slides for this workshop are included at the end of this chapter.

- projector, screen, and computer for displaying PowerPoint slides; alternatively, overhead transparencies and overhead projector

- flipchart and markers

- pens or pencils for each participant

- name badges for each participant

- handouts of slide presentation for each participant

- assorted toys and puzzles for the participant tables

- snacks and candy as desired.

Sample Agenda

8:00 a.m.   Welcome (10 minutes)

As participants enter the room, have slide 7–1 showing on the screen. Welcome them and introduce yourself. Allow each person to stand and give a brief introduction. Explain that the purpose of the workshop is to give them an overview of the skills and competencies that are most important to managers and to introduce them to the concepts of knowledge management, which allows them to share their expertise of these skills with others.

Explain the ground rules for the session. Here are some sample ground rules and housekeeping items:

- Silence cell phones. (It's a good practice to perform this action on your own cell phone at this time. It demonstrates leading by example and allows you to ensure that your phone isn't the one that rings during the session.)

◆ Explain that this workshop is interactive. Attendees are invited to participate and ask questions.

◆ Restrooms, smoking areas, snacks, and vending machines are located in the following areas: *[add details]*.

◆ Respectful communication is required. If someone is speaking, all attention should be given to that person.

8:10   Objectives and Agenda (5 minutes)

Show slide 7–2. Review the workshop objectives from the slide. The basic understanding is that this course serves as an overview of topics that will help them determine areas for their continuing development on the subjects addressed.

Show slide 7–3. Go through the agenda items and ask for any questions.

8:15   Manager Skills Overview (15 minutes)

Show slide 7–4. Ask them to think about a great manager they've worked with or heard about. Label a flipchart page: "Best Manager Traits" and ask participants to call out the traits that made this manager so great. What did this person do well? List these on the flipchart and ask them to list them on their handouts.

Show slide 7–5. Note that the traits they identified fall into different competency or skill categories. The manager skills on this slide are samples from competency listings used by organizations to assess and develop the skills of their managers.

These skills can be grouped even further, because they deal with one of two basic areas. Ask them if they can figure out the two main things managers handle by looking at the list of skills required. You can help them discover that the two focus areas are people and tasks. Show slide 7–6.

Quite often managers are stronger in one of these areas than the other. With development activities, they can develop the other skill area to become more effective in their roles.

Show slide 7–7. Dealing with people is called interpersonal skills, people skills, or soft skills. Ask if they can think of specific skill examples. Title your flipchart page "Interpersonal Skills" and list their ideas. Add to the list any of these that they don't mention: communication, coaching, presentation, facilitation, motivating, resolving conflicts, and working with customer-service situations.

Show slide 7–8. Title a flipchart page "Functional Skills." Note that the rest of the activities deal with tasks, including processes and information systems. These are sometimes referred to as functional, operational, or hard skills. Ask if they can think of examples of these. List their ideas and add to the list any of these that they don't mention: technological skills, performance management, time management, project management, records management, legal analysis, financial management, and problem solving.

8:30   Performance Management (10 minutes)

Show slide 7–9. Explain that the next segment will address the stages of performance management. Distribute Tool 12–16 and discuss these main phases of the performance management cycle.

Performance management starts with the planning stage in which the manager works with the employee to prepare him or her for the work that will be performed. During this stage managers will work to ensure that their employees understand their job responsibilities, their goals, and how their performance will be measured.

The performance stage is the actual period of work produced and all coaching for improvement that managers do throughout the year. During this stage, managers are expected to observe operations, conduct coaching sessions, address performance problems, and recognize and reward achievements.

The review stage is when managers and employees look back to evaluate the year's accomplishments and challenges. In this final stage of performance management, managers review the accomplishments and challenges of employees, evaluate the performance of each employee, schedule and conduct individual performance appraisal sessions, and set goals and timelines for the upcoming performance period.

And with this, the cycle starts over again.

8:40   Knowledge Management (10 minutes)

Show slide 7–10. Introduce this segment by asking if there has ever been a time that a process has had to be postponed because the person in the office who normally handled that procedure was out. Ask what effect this had on productivity.

Explain that knowledge management seeks to eliminate problems such as department stalls due to absent employees and the loss of knowledge that occurs when a long-time employee retires. Knowledge management is the range of practices that businesses use to identify and share knowledge across the organization. These include practices such as cross-training, job shadowing, training classes, intranet resources, and company databases.

Show slide 7–11. Distribute Tool 12–19. Give a basic overview of knowledge management and how it can benefit their workplaces by explaining the following concepts:

◆ Career Path or Career Map: A predefined set of jobs or positions through which an employee might progress to achieve a desired level in the organization.

◆ Competency: The knowledge, skills, abilities (KSAs) and behaviors that contribute to successful performance in a particular position or occupational level.

◆ Individual Development Plan (IDP): A document that includes an assessment of an employee's current skills and an outline of how the employee will develop the knowledge, skills, and abilities to meet the organization's changing needs and to achieve future career goals.

◆ Succession Planning: A process designed to create talent pools and learning opportunities to ensure that potential successors are identified and developed to fill key roles in the organization.

◆ Types of Organizational Knowledge: *Explicit knowledge* is knowledge of company procedures and processes that can be tracked in manuals, directories, and other references. *Tacit knowledge* is estimated to make up 80 to 85 percent of an organization's knowledge assets. It's composed of people's insight, judgment, and know-how, which requires more interpersonal training methods, such as coaching and mentoring. Ask participants if they can think of some examples of tacit knowledge within their own departments.

◆ Workforce Planning: The process of analyzing the current workforce, identifying future workforce needs, and developing solutions to address the gaps that exist between those two.

Show slide 7–12. Distribute Training Instrument 12–17 and Tool 12–20 and note that these forms can help attendees discover the management skills they'd like to focus on developing. When they return to the workplace, they can use this information in a discussion with their managers so they can work together to determine SMART goals (specific, measurable, achievable, relevant, and time-bound).

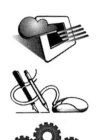

8:50   Question-and-Answer Session (5 minutes)

Show slide 7–13. Open the floor to questions. Use this as an opportunity to promote any manager development sessions that you have scheduled.

8:55   Evaluations (5 minutes)

Show slide 7–14. Remind them that, just as they are doing with their manager skills, you want to continue developing your skills. So, now you'd like their ideas for improvement by their comments on the final evaluation form. Distribute Assessment 12–2 and ask them to complete these before they leave.

Show slide 7–15. Thank them for their attention and end with a motivating story, quote, or anecdote from your collection.

9:00   Adjourn

What to Do Next

◆ Using the material in chapter 4 as a guide, build a detailed plan to prepare for this workshop.

◆ Schedule a training room and invite your attendees.

◆ Draft a supply list, teaching notes, and time estimates.

◆ Decide how you will support the action plan to which your learners will commit.

◆ Evaluate the effectiveness of the program, using the ideas from chapter 6.

◆ Consider designing follow-up sessions to encourage the learners to continue developing manager skills.

Slide 7-1

Slide 7-2

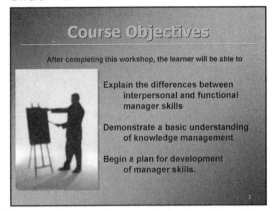

Slide 7-3

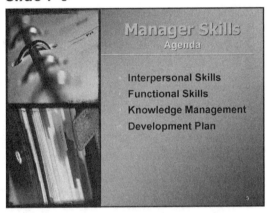

Slide 7-4

Slide 7-5

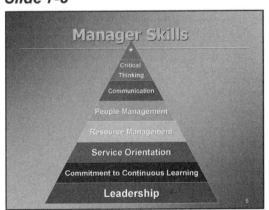

Slide 7-6

Slide 7-7

Slide 7-8

Slide 7-9

Slide 7-10

Slide 7-11

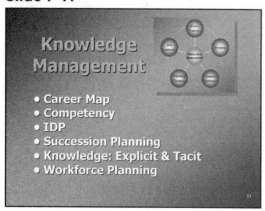

Slide 7-12

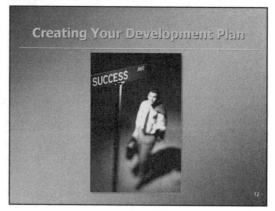

Slide 7-13

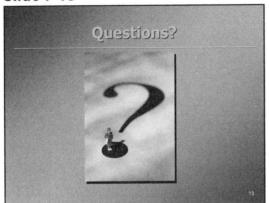

Slide 7-14

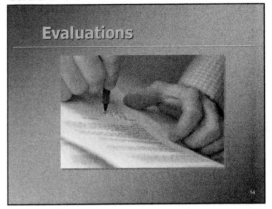

Slide 7-15

◆

Half-Day Program

- Objectives for the half-day manager skills workshop
- Lists of materials for facilitator and participants
- Detailed program agenda to be used as a facilitator's guide

The half-day workshop allows learners to address both interpersonal and functional manager skills. The first section of the workshop focuses on the interpersonal or soft skills. During the second half of the workshop, emphasis is on the functional or hard competencies that a manager needs to master. The half-day workshop enables attendees to participate in either discussions or practice sessions of the skills in each section by adjusting the time allowed for activities, so please note the changes in time allotment for the Learning Activities and use the ones listed in the following sample agenda. At the end of the workshop, learners will create an action plan for continued development.

Training Objectives

The participants' objectives for the half-day manager skills workshop are to be able to

- use interpersonal skills for improved business communications
- employ functional skills for greater efficiency with tasks and processes
- establish a plan for continued development of management skills.

Materials

For the facilitator:

- this chapter for reference and use as a facilitator guide
- Learning Activity 11–1: Introductions

- Learning Activity 11–16: Legal Issues

- Learning Activity 11–20: Development Plan

- Assessment 12–1: Manager Self-Assessment

- Assessment 12–2: Evaluation Form

- Training Instrument 12–6: Presentation Skills

- Training Instrument 12–13: Legal Issues

- Training Instrument 12–17: Development Plan

- Tool 12–1: Coaching Steps

- Tool 12–2: Conflict Management Strategies

- Tool 12–3: Presentation Design Form

- Tool 12–10: Time Management

- Tool 12–16: Performance Management Process

- Tool 12–19: Knowledge Management

- Tool 12–20: Individual Development Plan

- PowerPoint slide program, titled "Manager Skills" (slides 8–1 through 8–32). To access slides for this program, open the file *Half-day.ppt* on the website. Thumbnail versions of the slides for this workshop are included at the end of this chapter.

- projector, screen, and computer for displaying PowerPoint slides; alternatively, overhead transparencies and overhead projector

- flipchart and markers

- pens or pencils for each participant

- name badges for each participant

- three-ring binder for each participant

- sticky notes attached to the front of each binder

- assorted toys and puzzles for the participant tables

- snacks and candy as desired

Sample Agenda

8:00 a.m. Welcome (5 minutes)

As participants enter the room, have slide 8–1 showing on the screen. Welcome them and ask them to use a sticky note from the front of their binders to write one of the main challenges they face as a manager. If they're new managers, they can write one area about which they are most concerned. Once they've written their notes, instruct them to attach them to the "What Do I Need From This Workshop?" flipchart page displayed at the front of the room.

Introduce yourself and summarize the *What Do I Need?* notes on the flipchart. Explain that the purpose of the workshop is to introduce tools and techniques that will help them deal with these challenges. Today also allows them to step out of the daily rush and focus on the skills they'd like to develop for their roles as managers. If you have experienced managers in the group, this is a good time to note that it's impressive to see managers with varying levels of seniority in this workshop, because that illustrates one of the most important lessons you'll be discussing today. That lesson is the example that managers set by being willing to continue learning and being open to new ideas. Their example helps their employees accept coaching and development ideas in a positive light.

Explain the ground rules for the session. Here are some sample ground rules and housekeeping items:

♦ Silence cell phones. (It's a good practice to perform this action on your own cell phone at this time. It demonstrates leading by example and allows you to ensure that your phone isn't the one that rings during the session.)

♦ Emphasize that this workshop is interactive. Be prepared to participate!

♦ There will be scheduled breaks during the session.

♦ Restrooms, smoking areas, snacks, and vending machines are located in the following areas: *[add details]*.

♦ Respectful communication is required. If someone is speaking, all attention should be given to that person.

8:05   Objectives (5 minutes)

Show slide 8–2. Review the workshop objectives from the slide. The basic understanding should be that a number of subjects will be addressed during the course of this workshop, and participants are not expected to be experts in all of them by the end of the session. This course serves as an overview of tools and techniques that will help them in their continuing development on the subjects addressed.

8:10   Agenda (5 minutes)

Show slide 8–3. Go through the agenda items and ask for any questions.

8:15   Introductions (15 minutes)

Show slide 8–4. Perform the activity as described in Learning Activity 11–1: Introductions. Once you've completed the activity, refer to the flipchart pages and note that you now have a good starter list of manager skills to focus on today, but there are many more. Explain that this next activity will allow them to look at other skills that they'll want to develop.

8:30   The Best Manager I Ever Knew . . . (10 minutes)

Show slide 8–5. Ask them to think about a great manager they've worked with or heard about. Label a flipchart page "Best Manager Traits" and ask attendees to call out the traits that made this manager so great. What did this person do well? List these on the flipchart and ask them to list them on their handouts. This discussion sets the stage for the following assessment of manager skills.

You can transition to this assessment by noting that many of the skills and traits needed to be a successful manager are represented in this room. The following assessment will help them discover their strongest skill areas and give them some ideas of skills they can develop.

8:40   Self-Assessment (15 minutes)

Show slide 8–6. Distribute Assessment 12–1. Ask learners to complete this assessment individually. Assure them that the answers they give are for their eyes only, so they can be completely candid.

When everyone is finished, briefly discuss the questions on the assessment. Ask if they discovered areas that they would like to develop. Allow volunteers to share some of the areas in which they feel strong. Ask if anyone wants to share areas for development that he or she has discovered, but do not force participants to respond. Explain that the materials offered in today's workshop are designed to help them in each of those areas.

Show slide 8–7. The manager skills listed on this slide are samples from competency listings used by organizations to assess and develop the skills of their managers.

8:55   The Roles of the Manager . . . (10 minutes)

Show slide 8–8. Ask learners to call out the different activities a manager is expected to perform each day. Use a flipchart to list these. You can get them started by mentioning one or two examples, such as handling payroll or interviewing potential employees.

Once you have a list of activities, ask them to help you sort these into two groups. Use a colored marker to circle the items that use interpersonal skills, often called people skills or soft skills. Note that the rest of the activities deal with tasks, including processes and information systems.

These are sometimes referred to as functional, or hard skills. Refer back to the flipchart pages posted around the room that detail other manager skills to demonstrate that the same is true of those lists.

Those are the two basic responsibilities of managers—dealing with people and dealing with tasks. Explain that, in this workshop, they'll practice their skills in both of these areas.

9:05   Interpersonal Skills . . . (15 minutes)

Show slide 8–9. Introduce this section by noting that you'll start the day by concentrating on people skills, or interpersonal communication techniques. Because many of the roles they have discussed dealt with handling emotions, conflict, and change in the workplace, it is essential that managers be able to communicate clearly and effectively. The first part of the workshop will give them an opportunity to determine their level of success with their communication skills and how they can continue to make those skills more effective.

Show slide 8–10. Remind them that the best communication skill we can practice is the one we can do without saying a word. Listening. But not just any listening will do. It must be active listening. Ask them to compare the kind of listening they do when they listen to television commercials with the kind of listening they do when a doctor is giving them instructions on how to take their medicine. Is it the same? One hopes not.

Active listening is the kind of listening managers need to develop, and it's a hard skill to maintain with all the distractions of the workplace. Go to the flipchart and write the title: "Active Listening." Ask them for examples of things they do that indicate they are actively listening to someone. To get them started you can mention such activities as nodding, maintaining eye contact, taking notes, ignoring the phone, turning away from the computer, summarizing, asking questions, making listening noises, and using body language.

List these ideas on the page as they call them out and ask them to make note of these on their handouts, so they can make an effort to incorporate more of these skills into their daily interactions. Remove this page from the flipchart and post it so that it stays visible throughout the day, and you can add other notes or suggestions as they are mentioned.

Show slide 8–11: Communication Skills. Title a flipchart page: "Communications." Discuss the three parts of oral communication: words, tone, and body language. Create a column for each of these on the flipchart page.

Conduct a quick demonstration of how these need to work together by showing a negative example. Cross your arms, look stern, and say angrily, "I really hope you're having a nice day."

Ask what the problem with this communication is. After they have brought up your tone and body language, agree and follow up by noting how often managers send these same kinds of conflicting messages. For example, a manager might say he or she is listening to an employee, but presents a different message if he or she is checking emails while the employee talks.

Ask for ways that managers can be more effective with their words, tone, and body language and list them in the appropriate column on the flipchart page, instructing participants to add these notes to their handouts.

Examples of words would include using positive language, appropriate vocabulary, and avoiding acronyms until after you have explained them to the listener.

Examples of tone would include being aware of mood, taking time to calm down so that tone is even and relaxed, speaking at an appropriate volume, avoiding a condescending or sarcastic tone, and being upbeat in communications.

Examples of body language might include maintaining eye contact; smiling; leaning toward the person; and avoiding negative body language such as tapping their feet, looking at their watches, sighing, or grimacing.

Explain that they will discuss how to use these interpersonal skills in coaching situations when they return from the 15-minute break.

9:20   Break (15 minutes)

9:35   Coaching Skills (15 minutes)

Show slide 8–12. Note that, if they observe the words, tone, and body language of their employees, they are going to discover opportunities for coaching and feedback. Additionally, there are many other times they'll need to use coaching skills. Title a flipchart page: "Coaching Opportunities." Ask for examples of times when they'll need to coach, teach, or counsel employees. Among the answers you can offer to get them started are

- ◆ when a person is new to a position

- ◆ when a person takes on new duties

- ◆ when someone is going on vacation and needs a back-up worker

- ◆ when someone is showing signs of frustration

- ◆ when mistakes are made

- ◆ when an employee is procrastinating because he or she doesn't know how to do something

- ◆ when the employee asks for help.

Suggest that they list these items on their handouts. This list offers just a few of the times when coaching and feedback may be called for. Remind them that they don't have to wait for a problem to appear to coach employees. Coaching individuals to help their growth and development is an important responsibility of a manager and ensures that employees do not equate all coaching sessions with negative feedback.

Distribute Tool 12–1. Explain that this tool allows them to ask the right questions to design a coaching session.

To make the most of these coaching opportunities, suggest that managers make use of the guidelines for effective coaching. You can solicit their ideas on each of these actions and summarize with the following notes for before, during, and after a coaching session.

Show slide 8–13. These are the things a manager should do before a coaching session.

- ◆ Observe—Often called MBWA (managing by walking around), this is the best way for a manager to stay in touch with what is going on in his or her department. If problems or areas for development are observed, this gives the manager an opportunity to look into these before they become major issues.

- ◆ Schedule time for coaching—Although many coaching sessions can be impromptu and informal events, major coaching sessions should be scheduled so that time is available to adequately address the subject. Coaching sessions should not be rushed.

- ◆ Prepare for coaching discussions—Managers should do their homework before coaching sessions. If it is a corrective action session, the manager needs to have done research and gathered specific information on the situation in advance of the meeting.

Show slide 8–14. Review the actions a manager can take to conduct an effective coaching session.

- ◆ Set a positive tone—The coaching session may concern a negative experience, but it doesn't have to take a negative tone. Start the session by stating the positive outcomes that are expected and spotlight the employee's strengths in other areas. This will ensure that the person is not immediately on the defensive.

◆ Define the issue—It is important to clearly and objectively state the issue to be discussed so that misunderstandings do not occur. Stick to this single issue.

◆ Listen—Listening can be the most important element in a coaching session. An employee may need to vent, explain, or confirm that he or she understands the topic that is being addressed. Allowing the employee to vent is an effective way to get past the emotions that may prohibit progress, as long as it does not go on for too long and turn into a "gripe session."

◆ Conduct two-way communication—A coaching conversation can become negative quickly if a person feels he or she is being lectured to. Explaining the situation and its consequences in the workplace is vital, just as allowing input from the person is necessary to ensure the open exchange of information.

◆ Determine the solution (if the session is corrective feedback)—Allow the person to give ideas first. Allowing him or her to have input will help the employee accept the resolution to the situation.

◆ Use the TLC process of training (if the session is developmental)—T = Teach the process or information. L = Listen as the process is explained or demonstrated. C = Coach the individual on any adjustments he or she needs to make.

◆ Ask for feedback—Ask how the person feels about the solution reached or the process learned. Allow the person to ask questions.

◆ Set a timeframe for follow-up—Decide when you will get back together to revisit this coaching topic.

Show slide 8–15. These are the steps a manager will want to take following a coaching session.

◆ Follow up—Meet as scheduled to review progress, make additional adjustments, address continuing issues, or move to the next level of development.

◆ Recognize accomplishments—This is an excellent opportunity to recognize the development of this employee. Use reward and recognition practices if appropriate.

Remind the participants that, no matter how good their coaching and interpersonal skills are, conflict is normal in any workplace. Distribute Tool 12–2 and explain that this lists conflict management strategies they may find useful in those difficult situations.

9:50   Presentation Skills (35 minutes)

Show slide 8–16. Note that the parts of a presentation include the introduction, the main points, and the conclusion. Distribute Tool 12–3. Attendees will be able to use this format to create presentations. You can briefly walk them through this form by referring to the instructions in each section.

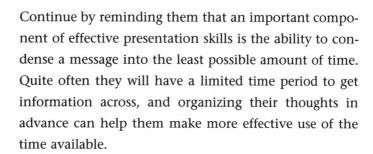

Continue by reminding them that an important component of effective presentation skills is the ability to condense a message into the least possible amount of time. Quite often they will have a limited time period to get information across, and organizing their thoughts in advance can help them make more effective use of the time available.

Show slide 8–17. Distribute Training Instrument 12–6. Explain that the SET formula is used to get the answer to a question across in the shortest time available, such as the time necessary for an average elevator ride. That's why it's often called an elevator speech. SET stands for the Short Answer, Evidence supporting that short answer, and the Transition, which includes a summary statement and handing the floor back to another person.

Demonstrate an example of this such as this quick answer to the question, "What is an elevator speech?" "An elevator speech is a talk that can be given in 30 to 60 seconds, which is the time span of an average elevator ride. It uses the SET formula of Short Answer, Evidence supporting the short answer, and Transition or summary statement, and it allows you to give a complete presentation in a limited amount of time. Any questions?"

Explain that now you'll allow them to practice the elevator speech and conduct their own review. Their assignment is to take anything they have learned this morning and condense it into a review of less than 60 seconds. Give them five minutes to do this. Then allow each person to present his or her "mini review."

10:25   Time Management Concepts (30 minutes)

Show slide 8–18. Introduce this section to participants by explaining that you'd like to start this discussion on time management by looking at how they manage their days. Ask for a show of hands of how many attendees use a planning system every day. Ask how many of them feel that they are effective in the management of their time. If not, assure them that they're not alone. There's a reason that so many time management systems, software packages, books, and classes exist today. We all have challenges in managing the events and tasks of our lives. Show slide 8–19. Distribute Tool 12–10. Review the basics of time management as shown on the slide.

- ◆ Use only one system. Ask how many of them use multiple systems, such as Outlook, a PDA, the cell phone organizer, a notebook, or even the refrigerator door at home to track different events and activities. Ask if they can see what the problem might be with this. The answer is that there's only one of each of them and there's only one 5:00 p.m. each day. So, if they have their child's soccer game listed on the refrigerator door at home and they're still at work at 5:00 p.m., what's going to happen? Right. They now have an angry child. Keeping all appointments, professional and private, in one location eliminates this possibility. If they're uncomfortable with having their private appointments listed in this book, suggest they create their own codes for them.

◆ Monitor and track progress throughout the day. This means checking off items as they are completed, making note of start and stop times of activities, and even making notes of interruptions. This will not only help them analyze the areas in which they need to make adjustments, but will help them when they return from an interruption, because they can look at their notes to see what they were working on before they were called away.

◆ Schedule planning time every day. It might be in the morning before anyone else gets into the office. It might be in the evening as they review their accomplishments for the day. No matter what the time, this session should include a review of the day's tasks to see which were completed or deleted, and scheduling of those that need to be completed on another day.

◆ Prioritize. Many of us have a tendency to do the easy tasks first and keep putting off the more involved activities. Instead, remind them that they need to use the daily planning session to prioritize and determine the most important activities and those with impending deadlines. Scheduling those first will ensure they meet goals, and those smaller tasks can be scheduled around the more important ones.

◆ Be flexible. Remind them that interruptions will still occur. Firefighting will still be necessary. But advance planning will help them ensure that when they get back from firefighting, they're ready to jump right back in on the highest priority task on their list.

Tell them you want their help in examining prioritization a little more closely.

Divide the class into three groups. Assign one of the levels of prioritization to each group. Allow them to discuss this level for seven minutes and come up with some examples of types of activities they would include in this prioritization level.

Explain the A group's level of prioritization and then ask that group to share their findings. Do the same for the Bs, and Cs of prioritization.

At this point you can tell them that you'd like to take a moment to test their knowledge on a very important topic that a lot of managers have problems with. It's the legal side of management.

10:55   Legal Issues (15 minutes)

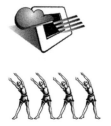

Show slide 8–20. Perform the activity as described in Learning Activity 11–16: Legal Issues. Adjust the time from the suggested 25 minutes to 15 minutes by allowing five minutes for them to answer questions and 10 minutes for discussion. Allow time for additional discussion if you are ahead of schedule. Groups normally get animated during this discussion because they are surprised by answers or share their related experiences. Don't be surprised if questions come up in this section that you can't answer. Laws change, interpretations are different, and there are many legal variations that exist, based on your location. And you never want to try to guess when it comes to legal issues! Just make a list of any questions that you weren't sure about so you can research them and email the group with answers later.

Summarize the legal discussion by showing slide 8–21 and reviewing a few basics.

◆ It's the impact of their actions, not the intent, that matters.

◆ Legal issues that are brought to them should never be handled carelessly or with disregard.

◆ The company, as well as the manager, can be held liable in legal complaints.

◆ The employee has a right to a safe, comfortable working environment. A manager should be aware of potential problems and address them in a timely manner.

◆ Laws change and new precedents are set every day. If workshop participants have the slightest doubt about an employee issue, they should talk to their human resources representative. And remind attendees that any employee harassment, violence, or other reports they receive should be forwarded to the HR department. Such a report should never stop with them.

Before you take a break, remind them of the exact time you need them back in their seats. Explain that the next section concerns performance management and an important aspect of performance management is getting to work on time!

11:10   Break (10 minutes)

11:20   Performance Management (15 minutes)

Show slide 8–22. Explain that the next segment will address the stages of performance management. Distribute Tool 12–16 and discuss the main phases of the performance management cycle.

Show slide 8–23 and explain the cycle of performance management.

Performance management starts with the planning stage, during which the manager works with the employee to prepare him or her for the work that will be performed. The performance stage refers to the actual performance of the work and coaching for improvement throughout the year. The review stage is looking back to evaluate the year's accomplishments and challenges. And then the cycle starts over again.

- ◆ Show slide 8–24. Planning—During this stage participants will work with their employees to ensure the employees understand their job responsibilities, their goals, and how their performance will be measured. To do this, they'll review job descriptions with their department members, create a development plan with goals and timelines, and review the performance appraisal form with employees.

- ◆ Show slide 8–25. Performance—During this stage, managers are expected to observe operations, conduct coaching sessions with their employees on both a formal and informal basis, and to address and guide the correction of performance problems. During this period the manager should also take the time to recognize and reward achievements.

- ◆ Show slide 8–26. Review—In the final stage of performance management, managers review the accomplishments and challenges of employees, evaluate the performance of each employee, schedule and conduct individual performance appraisal sessions, and set goals and timelines for the upcoming performance period. And with this, the cycle starts over again.

Transition to the next section by explaining that members of the organization can only perform effectively if they have the resources and knowledge they need for their positions. Managing that knowledge and information is a focus of forward-thinking organizations today. The next section will address knowledge management.

11:35   Knowledge Management (15 minutes)

Show slide 8–27. Introduce this segment by asking if there has ever been a time that a process has had to be postponed because the person in the office who normally handled that procedure was out. Ask what effect this had on staff productivity.

Show slide 8–28. Explain that knowledge management seeks to eliminate problems such as department stalls due to absent employees and the loss of knowledge that occurs when a long-time employee retires. Knowledge management consists of the range of practices that businesses use to identify and share knowledge across the organization. These include practices such as cross-training, job shadowing, training classes, intranet resources, and company databases.

Show slide 8–29. Distribute Tool 12–19. Give a basic overview of knowledge management and how it can benefit their workplaces by explaining the following concepts:

- Career Path or Career Map: A predefined set of jobs or positions through which an employee might progress to achieve a desired level in the organization.

- Competency: The knowledge, skills, abilities (KSAs) and behaviors that contribute to successful performance in a particular position or occupational level.

◆ Individual Development Plan (IDP): A document that includes an assessment of an employee's current skills and an outline of how the employee will develop the knowledge, skills, and abilities to meet the changing needs of the organization and to achieve future career goals.

◆ Succession Planning: A process designed to create talent pools and learning opportunities to ensure that potential successors are identified and developed to fill key roles in the organization.

◆ Types of Organizational Knowledge: Explicit knowledge is knowledge of company procedures and processes that can be tracked in manuals, directories, and other references. Tacit knowledge is estimated to make up 80 to 85 percent of an organization's knowledge assets. It's composed of people's insight, judgment, and know-how, which requires more interpersonal training methods, such as coaching and mentoring. Ask participants if they can think of some examples of tacit knowledge.

◆ Workforce Planning: The process of analyzing the current workforce, identifying future workforce needs, and developing solutions to address the gaps that exist between those two constitutes workforce planning.

11:50   Continued Development Action Plan (15 minutes)

Show slide 8–30. Inform learners that they are now ready for the most important part of any workshop: Determining how they will use the information they have received once they have returned to their positions as managers.

Perform the activity as listed in Learning Activity 11–20: Development Plan. They will focus on answering the questions on Training Instrument 12–17. When they return to the workplace, they can use this information in a discussion with their managers so they can work together to determine SMART goals (specific, measurable, achievable, relevant, and time-bound) and action steps as indicated on Tool 12–20.

12:05 Question-and-Answer Session (10 minutes)

Show slide 8–31. Open the floor to questions. Also, take this opportunity to look at the sticky notes from the beginning of the session to ensure that all the challenges learners presented have been addressed. Don't worry if you can't answer all of the questions. There's always something that catches us unaware in these sessions! If you don't know, tell them you'll find out and get back in touch with them. If everyone wants to know the information, you can send a follow-up email to the entire group and include reminders from the session. It's a great way to keep the workshop information fresh in their minds.

12:15 Evaluations (5 minutes)

Show slide 8–32. Remind them that, just as they are doing with their manager skills, you want to continue developing your skills. So, now you'd like their ideas for improving the workshop through suggestions given on the final evaluation form. Distribute Assessment 12–2 and ask them to complete these before they leave.

Show slide 8–33. Thank them for their attention and end with a motivating story, quote, or anecdote from your collection.

12:20 Adjourn

What to Do Next

◆ Using the material in chapter 4 as a guide, build a detailed plan to prepare for this workshop.

◆ Schedule a training room and invite your attendees.

◆ Draft a supply list, teaching notes, and time estimates.

◆ Decide how you will support the action plan to which your learners will commit.

◆ Evaluate the effectiveness of the program, using the ideas from chapter 6.

◆ Consider designing follow-up sessions to encourage the learners to continue developing manager skills.

Slide 8-1

Slide 8-2

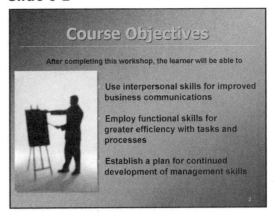

Slide 8-3

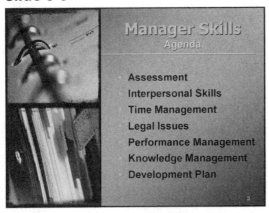

Slide 8-4

Slide 8-5

Slide 8-6

Slide 8-7

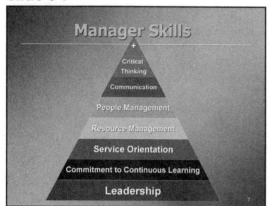

Slide 8-8

Slide 8-9

Slide 8-10

Slide 8-11

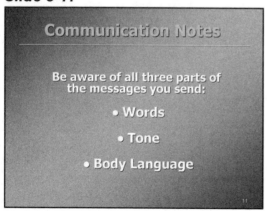

Slide 8-12

Slide 8-13

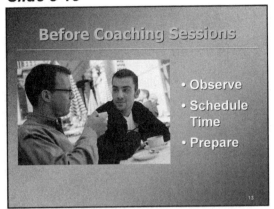

Slide 8-14

Slide 8-15

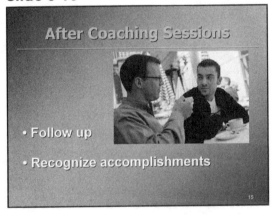

Slide 8-16

Slide 8-17

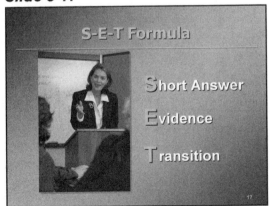

Slide 8-18

Slide 8-19

Time Management

- Use only one system
- Monitor and track progress throughout the day
- Schedule planning time every day
- Prioritize
- Be flexible

Slide 8-20

Slide 8-21

Basic Concepts

It's the impact of actions, not the intent, that matters.

Every employee has the right to feel safe and comfortable in his or her work environment.

Any report you receive should be communicated to your HR representative.

Slide 8-22

Slide 8-23

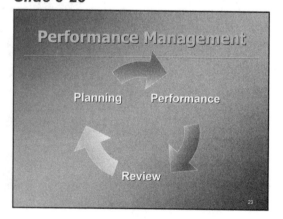

Slide 8-24

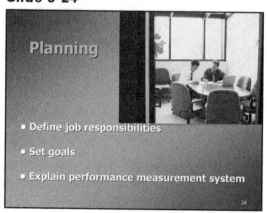

Slide 8-25

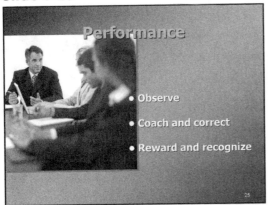

Slide 8-26

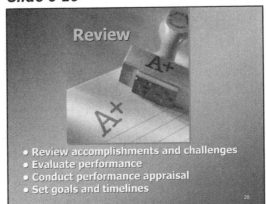

Slide 8-27

Slide 8-28

Slide 8-29

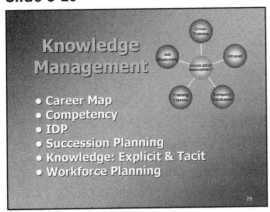

Slide 8-30

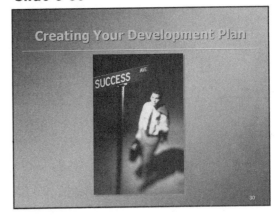

Slide 8-31

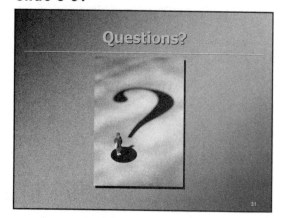

Slide 8-32

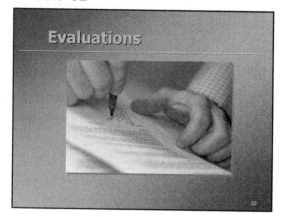

Slide 8-33

One-Day Program

- Objectives for the one-day manager skills workshop
- Lists of materials for facilitator and participants
- Detailed program agenda to be used as a facilitator's guide

The one-day workshop provides time for learners to address both interpersonal and functional manager skills. The first half day of the workshop focuses on the interpersonal or soft skills. During the second half of the workshop, emphasis is on the functional or hard competencies that a manager needs to master. The one-day workshop enables attendees to participate in either discussion or practice of the skills in each section. At the end of the workshop, learners will create an action plan for continued development.

Training Objectives

The participants' objectives for the one-day manager skills workshop are to be able to

- use interpersonal skills for improved business communications
- employ functional skills for greater efficiency with tasks and processes
- establish a plan for continued development of management skills.

Materials

For the facilitator:

- this chapter for reference and use as a facilitator guide
- Learning Activity 11–1: Introductions

- ◆ Learning Activity 11–2: The Best Manager I Ever Knew . . .

- ◆ Learning Activity 11–4: Coaching Session Dos and Don'ts

- ◆ Learning Activity 11–6: Resolving Conflict

- ◆ Learning Activity 11–12: To Tell the Truth! Review

- ◆ Learning Activity 11–16: Legal Issues

- ◆ Learning Activity 11–20: Development Plan

- ◆ Assessment 12–1: Manager Self-Assessment

- ◆ Assessment 12–2: Evaluation Form

- ◆ Training Instrument 12–1: The Best Manager I Ever Knew . . .

- ◆ Training Instrument 12–3: Coaching Skills

- ◆ Training Instrument 12–5: Resolving Conflict

- ◆ Training Instrument 12–13: Legal Issues

- ◆ Training Instrument 12–17: Development Plan

- ◆ Tool 12–1: Coaching Steps

- ◆ Tool 12–2: Conflict Management Strategies

- ◆ Tool 12–3: Presentation Design Form

- ◆ Tool 12–4: Agenda Form

- ◆ Tool 12–5: Meeting Planning Form

- ◆ Tool 12–6: Minutes Format

- ◆ Tool 12–8: Customer Service Formula

- ◆ Tool 12–10: Time Management

- ◆ Tool 12–11: Project Management

- ◆ Tool 12–16: Performance Management Process

- ◆ Tool 12–17: Performance Appraisals

- ◆ Tool 12–19: Knowledge Management

- ◆ Tool 12–20: Individual Development Plan

- PowerPoint slide program, titled "Manager Skills" (slides 9–1 through 9–51). To access slides for this program, open the file *One-Day.ppt* on the accompanying website. Thumbnail versions of the slides for this workshop are included at the end of this chapter.

- projector, screen, and computer for displaying PowerPoint slides; alternatively, overhead transparencies and overhead projector

- flipchart and markers

- pens or pencils for each participant

- name badges for each participant

- three-ring binder for each participant

- sticky notes attached to the front of each binder

- assorted toys and puzzles for the participant tables

- snacks and candy as desired.

Sample Agenda

8:00 a.m.   Welcome (5 minutes)

As participants enter the room, have slide 9–1 showing on the screen. Welcome them and ask them to use a sticky note from the front of their binders to write one of the main challenges they have as a manager. If they're new managers, they can write about a concern they have in becoming a manager. Once they've written their notes, instruct them to go up and attach them to the "What Do I Need From This Workshop?" flipchart page displayed at the front of the room.

Introduce yourself and explain that the purpose of the workshop is to introduce tools and techniques to help them in their roles as managers. If you have experienced managers in the group, this is a good time to note that it's impressive to see managers with varying levels of seniority in this workshop, because that illustrates one of the most important lessons you'll be discussing today, which is the example that managers set by being willing to continue learning and being open to new ideas. Their example helps their employees accept coaching and developmental ideas in a positive light.

Explain the ground rules for the session. Here are some sample ground rules and housekeeping items:

- Silence cell phones. (It's a good practice to perform this action on your own cell phone at this time. It demonstrates leading by example and allows you to ensure that your phone isn't the one that rings during the session.)

- Reinforce the point that this workshop is interactive. Be prepared to participate!

- There will be scheduled breaks in the morning and afternoon.

- There will be a one-hour break for lunch.

- Restrooms, smoking areas, snacks, and vending machines are located in the following areas: *[add details]*.

- Respectful communication is required. If someone is speaking, all attention should be given to that person.

If participants don't know the area, it's a good idea to have maps to nearby restaurants or menus they can use to order lunch.

8:05   Objectives (5 minutes)

Show slide 9–2. Review the workshop objectives from the slide. The basic understanding should be that a number of subjects will be addressed during the course of this workshop, and they are not expected to be experts in all of them by the end of the day. This course serves as an overview of tools and techniques that will help them in their continuing development on the subjects addressed.

8:10   Agenda (5 minutes)

Show slide 9–3. Go through the agenda items and ask for any questions.

8:15   What Do I Need From This Workshop? (5 minutes)

Show slide 9–4. Read the sticky notes from the flipchart and assure attendees that the program will address those topics. You'll be able to refer to these as you close each topic to ensure that related questions have been answered. If any of the topics listed aren't discussed, you can add them to the question-and-answer (Q&A) period at the end of the workshop.

8:20   Introductions (15 minutes)

Show slide 9–5. Perform the activity as described in Learning Activity 11–1: Introductions. Once you've completed the activity, refer to the flipchart pages and note that you now have a good starter list of manager skills to focus on today, but there are many more. Explain that this next activity will allow them to look at other skills that they'll want to develop.

8:35   The Best Manager I Ever Knew . . . (20 minutes)

Show slide 9–6. Distribute Training Instrument 12–1. Perform the activity as described in Learning Activity 11–2: The Best Manager I Ever Knew . . . . This discussion sets the stage for an assessment of manager skills.

You can transition to this assessment by noting that many of the skills and traits of successful managers are represented in this room. The following assessment will help attendees discover the skills that are their strongest as well as give them some ideas of skills they can develop.

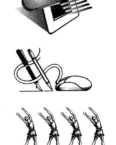

8:55   Self-Assessment (20 minutes)

Show slide 9–7. Distribute Assessment 12–1. Ask learners to complete this assessment individually. Assure them that the answers they give are for their eyes only, so they can be completely candid.

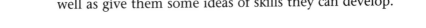

When everyone is finished, briefly discuss the questions on the assessment. Ask if they discovered areas that they would like to develop. Allow volunteers to share some of the areas in which they feel strong. Ask if anyone wants to share areas that they have discovered need development, but do not force them to respond. Explain that the materials in today's workshop are designed to help them in each of those areas.

Show slide 9–8. The manager skills on this slide are samples taken from competency listings used by organizations to assess and develop the skills of their managers.

9:15   The Roles of the Manager . . . (10 minutes)

Show slide 9–9. Ask learners to call out the different activities a manager performs each day. Use a flipchart to list these. You can get them started by mentioning one or two examples, such as handling payroll or interviewing potential employees.

Once you have a list of activities, ask them to help you sort these into two groups. Use a colored marker to circle the items that use interpersonal skills, often called people skills or soft skills. Note that the rest of the activities deal with tasks, including processes and information systems. These are sometimes referred to as functional, or hard skills. Refer back to the flipchart pages posted around the room that list other manager skills to demonstrate that the same is true of those lists.

Interpersonal and functional skills are the two basic responsibilities of managers—dealing with people and dealing with tasks. Explain that, in this workshop, they'll practice their skills in both of these areas.

9:25   Interpersonal Skills . . . (15 minutes)

Show slide 9–10. Introduce this section by noting that you'll start the day by concentrating on people skills, or interpersonal communication techniques. Because many of the roles they discussed dealt with handling emotions, conflict, and change in the workplace, it is essential that managers be able to communicate clearly and effectively. The first part of the workshop will give them an opportunity to determine their level of success with their communication skills and how they can continue to make those skills more effective.

Show slide 9–11. Remind them that the best communication skill we can practice is the one we can do without saying a word: Listening. But not just any listening will do. It must be active listening. Ask them to compare the kind of listening they do when they listen to television commercials with the kind of listening they do when a doctor is giving them instructions on how to take their medicine. Is it the same? One hopes not.

Active listening is the kind of listening managers need to develop, and it's a hard skill to maintain with all the distractions present in the workplace. Go to the flipchart and write the title: "Active Listening." Ask them for examples of things they do that indicate they are actively listening to someone. To get them started you can mention such activities as nodding, maintaining eye contact, taking notes, ignoring the phone, turning away from the computer, summarizing what they have heard, asking questions, making listening noises, and using body language.

List these ideas on the page as they call them out and ask them to make note of these on their handouts, so they can make an effort to incorporate more of these techniques into their daily interactions. Remove this page from the flipchart and post it so that it stays visible throughout the day, and you can add other notes or suggestions as they are mentioned.

Show slide 9–12: Communication Skills. Title a flipchart page: "Communications." Discuss the three parts of oral communication: words, tone, and body language. Create a column for each of these on the flipchart page.

Conduct a quick demonstration of how these need to work together by showing a negative example. Cross your arms, look stern, and say angrily, "I really hope you're having a nice day."

Ask what the problem with this communication is. After they have brought up your tone and body language, agree and follow up by noting how often managers send these same kinds of conflicting messages. For example, a manager might say he or she is listening to an employee, but presents a different message if he or she is checking emails while the employee is talking.

Ask for ways that managers can be more effective with their words, tone, and body language and list them in the appropriate column on the flipchart page, instructing participants to add these notes to their handouts.

Examples of words would include using positive language, appropriate vocabulary, and avoiding acronyms until after you have explained them to the listener.

Examples of tone would include being aware of mood, taking time to calm down so that tone is even and relaxed, speaking at an appropriate volume, avoiding a condescending or sarcastic tone, and being upbeat in communications.

Body language examples might include maintaining eye contact; smiling; leaning toward the person; and avoiding negative body language such as tapping their feet, looking at their watches, sighing, or grimacing.

Show slide 9–13 and ask for volunteers to summarize this section by reviewing a few ideas of how to be effective with each of the three parts of a message. These could be examples taken from the previous discussion or other ideas they have thought of.

Explain that they will get a chance to discover opportunities to use these interpersonal skills in coaching situations when they return from the 15-minute break.

9:40   Break (15 minutes)

9:55   Coaching Skills (15 minutes)

Show slide 9–14. Note that, if they observe the words, tone, and body language of their employees, they are going to discover opportunities for coaching and feedback. Additionally, there are many other times they'll need to use coaching skills. Title a flipchart page: "Coaching Opportunities." Ask for examples of times when they'll need to coach, teach, or counsel employees. Among the answers you can offer to get them started are

- ◆ when a person is new to a position

- ◆ when a person takes on new duties

- ◆ when someone is going on vacation and needs a backup

- ◆ when someone is showing signs of frustration

- ◆ when mistakes are made

- ◆ when an employee is procrastinating because he or she doesn't know how to do something

- ◆ when the employee asks for help.

These are just a few of the times when coaching and feedback may be called for. Remind them that they don't have to wait for a problem to appear to coach employees. Coaching individuals to help in their growth and development is an important managerial responsibility and ensures that employees do not equate all coaching sessions with negative feedback.

To make the most of these coaching opportunities, suggest that managers make use of the guidelines for effective coaching. You can solicit their ideas on each of these actions and summarize with the notes for before, during, and after a coaching session.

Show slide 9–15. These are the things a manager should do before a coaching session.

- Observe—Often called MBWA (managing by walking around), this is the best way for a manager to stay in touch with what is going on in his or her department. If problems or areas for development are observed, this gives the manager an opportunity to look into these before they become major issues.

- Schedule time for coaching—Although many coaching sessions can be impromptu and informal events, major coaching sessions should be scheduled so that time is available to adequately address the subject. Coaching sessions should not be rushed events.

- Prepare for coaching discussions—Managers should do their homework before coaching sessions. If it is a corrective action session, the manager needs to have done research and gathered specific information on the situation prior to the meeting.

Show slide 9–16. These are the actions a manager can take to conduct an effective coaching session.

- Set a positive tone—The coaching session may concern a negative experience, but it does not have to take a negative tone. Starting the session by stating the positive outcomes that are expected and spotlighting the employee's strengths in other areas can be ways to ensure that the person is not immediately put on the defensive.

- Define the issue—Clearly and objectively stating the issue to be discussed is important so that misunderstandings do not occur. Stick to this single issue.

◆ Listen—The most important thing a manager can do in a coaching session might be the act of listening to what the person being coached has to say. An employee may need to vent, explain, or confirm that he or she understands the topic that is being addressed. Allowing the employee to vent is an effective way to get past the emotions that may prohibit progress, as long as it does not go on for too long and turn into a "gripe session."

◆ Conduct two-way communication—A coaching conversation can become negative quickly if a person feels he or she is being lectured to. Explaining the situation and its consequences in the workplace is vital, just as allowing input from the person is necessary to ensure an open exchange of information.

◆ Determine the solution (if the session is corrective feedback)—Allow the person to give ideas first. Allowing him or her to have input will help with acceptance of the resolution to the situation.

◆ Use the TLC process of training (if the session is developmental)—T = Teach the process or information. L = Listen as the employee explains or demonstrates his or her understanding of the process. C = Coach him or her on any adjustments he or she needs to make.

◆ Ask for feedback—Ask how she or he feels about the solution reached or the process learned. Allow time for questions.

◆ Set a timetable for follow-up—Decide when you will get back together to revisit this coaching topic.

Show slide 9–17. These are the steps a manager will want to take following a coaching session.

- ◆ Follow up—Meet as scheduled to review progress, make additional adjustments, address continuing issues, or move to the next level of development.

- ◆ Recognize accomplishments—This is an excellent opportunity to recognize the development of this employee. Use reward and recognition practices if appropriate.

10:10   Coaching Skills Practice (20 minutes)

Show slide 9–18. Distribute Tool 12–1 and perform the activity as described in Learning Activity 11–4: Coaching Session Dos and Don'ts.

Summarize this topic by noting that, even with our best coaching skills, it is inevitable that there will be some conflict in a workplace. That's the next subject you'll cover.

10:30   Resolving Conflict (10 minutes)

Show slide 9–19. Start this section by telling the group that conflict in the workplace can be a good thing. Conflict is a natural result of diverse thinking, and it is this thinking that makes us question the status quo, consider new ideas, and develop innovative ways of improving outdated processes. It's when conflict is ignored, stifled, or allowed to escalate that problems arise.

Distribute Tool 12–2. Show slide 9–20. Compare the differences between good and bad conflict management, asking for their input as you discuss these points.

Bad conflict management includes avoiding conflict altogether. Ask them why this is the case. You might discuss how new ideas are never heard if the dominant people are never disagreed with. This lowers morale and can create a stagnant team.

Other conflict management issues include accepting the problem, or complaining rather than addressing the problem. This creates a negative atmosphere and they might find that other unrelated situations begin to be blamed on the conflict, as it becomes a scapegoat for the real issues that need to be addressed.

A final conflict management technique that is not always a good idea is discipline. Disciplining the team or taking punitive action may not address the actual reason the conflict exists and may only increase a divisive atmosphere among members of the team.

Show slide 9–21. Explain that good conflict management practices include addressing the conflicts in a timely manner and classifying them as learning opportunities. Even personality conflicts can teach you about how different team members operate and can help individuals learn to understand each other better.

Other good techniques include being flexible and creative in resolutions, setting ground rules so that all ideas can be shared without being criticized, and looking for win–win solutions. Interpersonal skills such as listening, using appropriate body language and tone, asking questions, using positive language, avoiding distractions, and resisting the urge to interrupt will also help in conflict situations.

Ask for learners' input on best practices that they have used in these types of situations.

Distribute Training Instrument 12–5. Ask the group to review the situation presented and help you brainstorm on ways to resolve this conflict. Remind them that a rule of brainstorming is that ideas are not judged. The goal is to list as many ideas as possible, concentrating on quantity, not quality.

Using a flipchart, list all the ideas offered. Once you have exhausted the list of ideas, discuss some of your favorite ideas from the list. Then, allow the group to choose their favorite ideas by a show of hands.

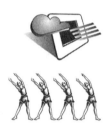

10:40   Resolving Conflict Activity (25 minutes)

Show slide 9–22. Perform the activity as described in Learning Activity 11–6: Resolving Conflict.

Remind them that, as you have discovered earlier today, miscommunication can come from conflicting interpersonal skills. An important interpersonal skill is our ability to communicate information clearly and in a positive manner. The next section will help develop that skill, whether the information is being presented to one person or to a large audience.

11:05   Presentation Skills (15 minutes)

Show slide 9–23. Note that the parts of a presentation include the introduction, the main points, and the conclusion. Distribute Tool 12–3. They will be able to use this format to create presentations. You can briefly walk them through this form by referring to the instructions in each section.

Continue by reminding them that an important component of effective presentation skills is the ability to condense a message so it is as succinct as possible. Quite often they will have a limited time period to get information across, and organizing their thoughts in advance can help them make more effective use of the time available.

Show slide 9–24. The SET formula is used to get the answer to a question across in the shortest time available, such as the period of an average elevator ride. That's why it's often called "an elevator speech." SET stands for the Short answer, Evidence supporting that short answer, and the Transition, which includes a summary statement and handing the floor back to another person.

Demonstrate an example of this such as offering this quick answer to the question, "What is an elevator speech?" "An elevator speech is a talk that can be given in 30 to 60 seconds, which is the time span of an average elevator ride. It uses the SET formula of Short answer, Evidence supporting the short answer, and a Transition or summary statement; an elevator speech allows you to give a complete presentation in a limited amount of time. Any questions?"

11:20   Effective Meetings (15 minutes)

Show slide 9–25. Allow them to read this humorous introduction to the topic of meetings. Ask them if this describes many of the meetings they attend. According to recent statistics, approximately 11 million meetings are held in the United States every day. That translates to about 37 percent of employee time being spent in meetings, according to the National Statistics Council. Additionally, researchers have found that 91 percent of meeting attendees admit to daydreaming during meetings, whereas 39 percent have actually dozed off.

Note that the way to make meetings an investment instead of a waste is to prepare for them. The most important steps your participants can take to conduct a successful meeting occur before anyone steps foot into the room.

Show slide 9–26. Explain that there are actions they need to take before, during, and afterward to ensure they conduct an effective meeting. Ask what they think are the necessary steps to take before the meeting. You can note that determining the invitees, creating the agenda, sending out communications, gathering background information, and planning the room layout can all help to make a meeting successful.

The steps that are taken during the meeting include posting the agenda, starting on time, using positive facilitation techniques, soliciting participation, and taking complete minutes.

After a meeting, evaluation is useful to determine what worked and what didn't. Also, sending out the minutes and action items with deadlines will remind attendees of what their next steps should be.

Distribute Tools 12-4, 12-5, 12-6 and briefly discuss the instructions in each section of the tools.

11:35   Customer Service Basics (15 minutes)

Show slide 9–27. Note that, when a manager is called in, it usually means that a customer service situation has hit a snag. The formula you're reviewing with them is a reminder of the basic steps necessary to resolving customer challenges.

Show slide 9–28. Distribute Tool 12–8. Discuss the steps of resolving customer challenges, including

- ◆ Listen—Sometimes a person just wants to know that his or her concern has been heard. Allowing the customer to vent can help reduce tension and set the stage for resolution.

- ◆ Apologize—This doesn't mean accepting blame. This simply means apologizing for the customer having had a negative experience.

- ◆ Conduct two-way conversation—This means asking questions, discussing, and listening to the customer to try to get to the root of the situation so that you can determine what the actual problem is that you are trying to resolve.

- ◆ Determine the solution together—Allow the customer to offer his or her possible solution first. Note that learners often find that the customer actually has a less extreme resolution than the one they're thinking of. And of course, you never want to tell the customer what you *can't* do.

Instead, reword your responses to tell what you *can* do.

- Explain what will happen next—Let the customer know exactly what steps will occur and the timeline for these steps.

- Thank them—Employees will want to end the conversation by thanking the customer for calling their attention to this situation and allowing them to be able to solve it instead of leaving the customer unhappy.

End the activity by opening the floor to questions and checking your flipchart page from the beginning of the class for additional questions on interpersonal skills. Remind them that the afternoon will be devoted to functional skills that will help them with the processes and procedures used in their workplaces. Break for lunch, being sure to tell them the exact time you need them back in their seats.

11:50	Lunch (60 minutes)
12:50	To Tell the Truth! (15 minutes)

Show slide 9–29. Perform the activity as described in Learning Activity 11–12: To Tell the Truth! Review

1:05   Time Management Concepts (20 minutes)

Show slide 9–30. Introduce this section to participants by explaining that you'd like to start this discussion on time management by looking at how they manage their days. Ask for a show of hands of how many attendees use a planning system every day. Ask how many of them feel that they are effective in the management of their time. If not, assure them that they're not alone. There's a reason that so many time-management systems, software packages, books, and classes exist today. We all have challenges in managing the events and tasks of our lives.

Write on a flipchart: "Time Wasters." Ask them what their biggest challenges to staying on schedule are. You'll get a variety of answers including the phone, email, people interrupting them, and crises. Acknowledge that all of these are a part of the job of manager. Without these interruptions, organizations might not even need managers! But by using a few select tools and guidelines, they will be able to more effectively manage both the interruptions and the scheduling of their time.

Show slide 9–31. Distribute Tool 12–10. These are the basics of any time management system.

- ◆ Use only one system. Ask how many of them use multiple systems, such as Outlook, a PDA, a cellphone organizer, a notebook, or even the refrigerator door at home to track different events and activities. Ask if they can see what the problem might be with this system. The answer is that there's only one of each of them and there's only one 5:00 p.m. each day. So, if they have their child's soccer game listed on the refrigerator door at home and they're still at work at 5:00 p.m., what's going to happen? Right. They now have an angry child. Keeping all appointments, professional and private, in one location eliminates this possibility. If they're uncomfortable with having their private appointments listed in this book, suggest they create their own codes for them.

- ◆ Monitor and track progress throughout the day. This means checking off items as they are completed, making note of start and stop times of activities, and even making notes of interruptions. This will not only help them analyze the areas in which they need to make adjustments, but will help them when they return from an interruption, because they can look at their notes to see what they were working on before they were called away.

- ◆ Schedule planning time every day. It might be in the morning before anyone else gets into the office. It might be in the evening as they review their accomplishments for the day. No matter what the time, this session should include a review of the day's tasks to see which were completed or deleted, and scheduling of those which need to be completed on another day.

◆ Prioritize. Many of us have a tendency to do the easy tasks first and keep putting off the more involved activities. Instead, remind them that they need to use their daily planning session to prioritize and determine the most important activities and those with impending deadlines. Scheduling those first will ensure they meet goals, and the smaller tasks can be scheduled around the more important ones.

◆ Be flexible. Remind them that interruptions will still occur. Firefighting will still be necessary. But advance planning will help them ensure that when they get back from firefighting, they're ready to jump right back in on the highest priority task on their list.

Show slide 9–32 and review the forms for scheduling and tracking daily activities. It's important to note that it doesn't matter what system they're using. It just needs to work for them. Some basics that they want to be sure are included in their system are listed on this slide.

The learners will need a planning calendar, so they can look at a glance to see what days are open. Since this calendar only has space blocked out with a general description of the event, they also need daily or weekly appointment pages to list details of those engagements. They need notes pages, either daily or weekly, to allow them to record all of their daily activities, meeting notes, and phone call information.

Other items are not as essential. Phone and contact lists are often kept on our phones or in our email databases, so having them in their planners can be optional. Sections for specific ongoing projects or clients can be useful if they will have numerous meetings and would like to keep all the information in one place. They can make their planner system as simple or elaborate as they wish. Once again, the main point is that they have to use it consistently to make it work for them.

1:25   Managing Projects (15 minutes)

Show slide 9–33. Explain to them that project management includes the same principles as time management, with the added dimension of more than one person working to get the tasks done.

Show slide 9–34. Distribute Tool 12–11. Review the chart with them to illustrate the basic concepts of project management.

The chart is simply populated with all the items that need to be accomplished to complete the project. But, since a task list without accountability or deadlines is going to be a list that won't get completed, they'll want to use all the additional columns recommended on this chart.

Invite them to try the basics of project management by telling them that you are going to put together a quick project. Choose a simple project such as painting a room, hosting a party, or something directly related to the group's occupation.

Write the project on a flipchart page. Now ask them to call out everything that has to be done to accomplish that project. Remind them that the order of task completion doesn't matter. This is a discussion that can get humorous or even loud as they call out ideas. You can let it go as far as you like if the group is experiencing an afternoon slump and needs an energizer.

Write down all ideas. Then, ask them to help you determine the order in which these tasks would need to occur.

Number them on the page. Explain that they have just created a project plan. They would simply take these tasks, put them into the project management chart, assign responsibilities and deadlines, and they are on their way to making this project happen.

In project management, tasks are created by brainstorming like this and then they are compiled into a list. The list is reviewed to determine the order in which tasks need to be completed. Then, they determine who will take ownership of each task, decide on deadlines, and assemble a list of resources that can help with the tasks.

By posting this chart, either physically in the office or on a shared database, the manager can keep the team's attention focused on the next steps of the project and offer a visual reminder to those who have deadlines coming up.

You can also note that other options available to track these tasks include various project management software programs or even using Microsoft Excel to create a simple version of a project management system.

At this point you can tell them that you'd like to take a moment to test their knowledge on a very important topic that a lot of managers have problems with. It's the legal side of management.

1:40   Legal Issues (25 minutes)

Show slide 9–35. Perform the activity as described in Learning Activity 11–16: Legal Issues. Allow time for discussion. Groups normally get animated during this discussion because they are surprised by answers or share their related experiences. Don't be surprised if questions come up in this section that you can't answer. Laws change, interpretations are different, and there are many variations based on your location. And you never want to try to guess when it comes to legal issues! Just make a list of any questions that you weren't sure about so you can research them and email the group with answers later.

Summarize the legal discussion by showing slide 9–36 and reviewing a few basics.

◆ It is the impact of their actions, not the intent, that matters.

◆ Legal issues that are brought to them should never be handled carelessly or with disregard.

◆ Not only the company, but the manager, can be held liable in legal complaints.

◆ The employee has a right to a safe, comfortable working environment. A manager should be aware of potential problems and address them in a timely manner.

◆ Laws change and new precedents are being set every day. If the manager has the slightest doubt about an employee issue, he or she should talk to the human resources representative. And remind attendees that any harassment, violence, or other employee report that they receive should be forwarded to the HR department. A report should never stop with them.

Before you take a break, remind them of the exact time you need them back in their seats. Explain that the next section concerns performance management and an important aspect of performance management is getting to work on time!

2:05   Break (15 minutes)

2:20   Performance Management (25 minutes)

Show slide 9–37. Explain that the next segment will address the stages of performance management. Distribute Tool 12–16 and discuss these main phases of the performance management cycle.

Show slide 9–38 and explain the cycle of performance management.

Performance management starts with the planning stage in which the manager works with the employee to prepare him or her for the work that will be performed. The performance stage is the actual performance of the work and coaching for improvement throughout the year. The review stage is looking back to evaluate the year's accomplishments and challenges. And then the cycle starts right back over again.

Explain that you'd like to study each of these stages in more detail. Divide participants into three groups and assign each group one of the three stages of performance management. They are to look at the upcoming slide on their handouts and brainstorm for five minutes to come up with reasons why that stage is important. Then each group will have five minutes to explain their stage and its importance.

◆ Show slide 9–39. Planning—During this stage they will work with their employees to ensure they understand their job responsibilities, their goals, and how their performance will be measured. To do this, they'll review job descriptions with their department members, create a development plan with goals and timelines, and review the performance appraisal form with employees.

◆ Show slide 9–40. Performance—During this stage, managers are expected to observe operations, conduct coaching sessions with their employees on both a formal and informal basis, and address and guide the correction of performance problems. During this period the manager should also take the time to recognize and reward achievements.

◆ Show slide 9–41. Review—In the final stage of performance management, managers review the accomplishments and challenges of employees, evaluate the performance of each employee, schedule and conduct individual performance appraisal sessions, and set goals and timelines for the upcoming performance period. And with this, the cycle starts over again.

Transition to the next section by explaining that, for many managers and employees, their least favorite aspect of performance management is the annual performance appraisal. That is the next section you'll discuss.

2:45   Appraisals (30 minutes)

Show Slide 9–42. Explain that the final step of performance management is the annual performance appraisal. This step is often dreaded, postponed, or rushed through by managers. It's not a comfortable activity for most managers, but the good news is it can actually be a positive experience if prepared and conducted with the employee's development in mind.

Show slide 9–43. Distribute Tool 12–17.

Divide the class into three groups or use the groups they are already in, if they worked well together on the previous discussion. Assign steps one through three to one group, steps four through six to another group, and steps seven to 10 to the third group.

Explain to the groups that they will have 10 minutes to discuss their steps and then present a five-minute explanation. They can use whatever method they want to explain their steps as a group, such as showing a demonstration, leading a panel discussion, or any creative method they might think of to get the points across.

3:15   Knowledge Management (15 minutes)

Show slide 9–44. Introduce this segment by asking if there has ever been a time that a process has had to be postponed because the person in the office who normally handled that procedure was out. Ask what effect this had on their productivity.

Show slide 9–45. Explain that knowledge management seeks to eliminate problems such as department stalls due to absent employees and the loss of knowledge that occurs when a long-time employee retires. Knowledge management consists of the range of practices that businesses use to identify and share knowledge across the organization. These include practices such as cross-training, job shadowing, training classes, intranet resources, and company databases.

Show slide 9–46. Distribute Tool 12–19. Give a basic overview of knowledge management and how it can benefit their workplaces by explaining these concepts:

- Career Path or Career Map: A predefined set of jobs or positions through which an employee might progress to achieve a desired level in the organization.

- Competency: The knowledge, skills, abilities (KSAs) and behaviors that contribute to successful performance in a particular position or occupational level.

- Individual Development Plan (IDP): A document that includes an assessment of an employee's current skills and an outline of how the employee will develop the knowledge, skills, and abilities to meet the changing needs of the organization and to achieve future career goals.

♦ Succession Planning: A process designed to create talent pools and learning opportunities to ensure that potential successors are identified and developed to fill key roles in the organization.

♦ Types of Organizational Knowledge: Explicit knowledge is knowledge of company procedures and processes that can be tracked in manuals, directories, and other references. Tacit knowledge, which is estimated to make up 80 to 85 percent of an organization's knowledge assets, is composed of people's insight, judgment, and know-how. Tacit knowledge requires more interpersonal training methods, such as coaching and mentoring. Ask participants if they can think of some examples of tacit knowledge.

♦ Workforce Planning: This involves the process of analyzing the current workforce, identifying future workforce needs, and developing solutions to address the gaps that exist between those two.

Show slide 9–47 and explain how an IDP is an excellent tool for both their employees and themselves. It helps the manager know what areas an employee needs to develop and what actions they are taking to improve their knowledge. It helps employees know what areas will help in their career development and guides their developmental efforts so they are focused on the right activities for their goals.

You can transition to the next segment by noting that now you'd like to give them the opportunity to develop their career paths and IDP.

3:30 Continued Development Action Plan (15 minutes)

Show slide 9–48. Distribute Tool 12–20. Inform learners that they are now ready for the most important part of any workshop. That part is determining how they will use the information they have received once they have returned to their positions as managers.

Perform the activity as listed in Learning Activity 11–20: Development Plan. They will focus on answering the questions on Training Instrument 12–17. When they return to the workplace, they can use this information in a discussion with their managers so they can work together to determine SMART goals (specific, measurable, achievable, relevant, and time-bound) and action steps.

3:45   Question-and-Answer Session (15 minutes)

Show slide 9–49. Open the floor to questions. Also, take this opportunity to look at the sticky notes from the beginning of the session to ensure that all the challenges presented have been addressed. Don't worry if you can't answer all of the questions. There's always something that catches us unaware in these sessions! If you don't know, tell them you'll find out the answer and get back in touch with them. If everyone wants to know the information, you can send a follow-up email to the entire group and include reminders from the session. It's a great way to keep the workshop information fresh in their minds.

4:00   Evaluations (10 minutes)

Show slide 9–50. Remind them that, just as they are doing with their managerial skills, you want to continue developing your skills. So, now you'd like their ideas for improving the workshop by getting their comments on the final evaluation form. Distribute Assessment 12–2 and ask them to complete these before they leave.

Show slide 9–51. Thank them for their attention and end with a motivating story, quote, or anecdote from your collection.

4:10   Adjourn

What to Do Next

◆ Using the material in chapter 4 as a guide, build a detailed plan to prepare for this workshop.

◆ Schedule a training room and invite your attendees.

◆ Draft a supply list, teaching notes, and time estimates.

◆ Decide how you will support the action plan to which your learners will commit.

◆ Evaluate the effectiveness of the program, using the ideas from chapter 6.

◆ Consider designing follow-up sessions to encourage learners to continue developing their managerial skills.

Slide 9-1

Slide 9-2

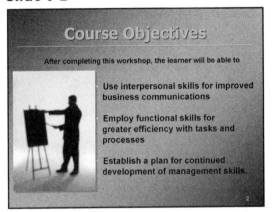

Slide 9-3

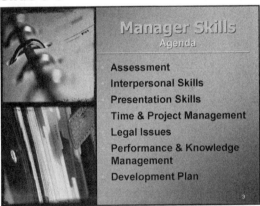

Slide 9-4

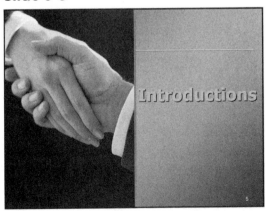

Slide 9-5

Slide 9-6

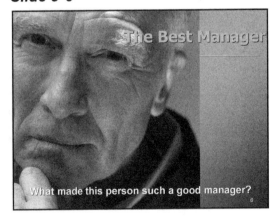

Slide 9-7

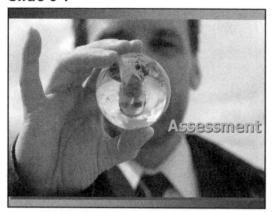

Slide 9-8

Slide 9-9

Slide 9-10

Slide 9-11

Slide 9-12

Slide 9-13

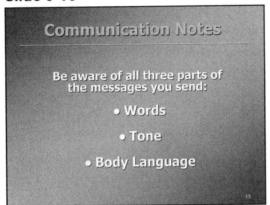

Slide 9-14

Slide 9-15

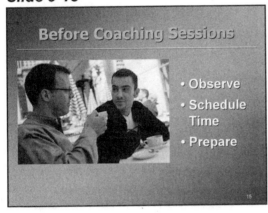

Slide 9-16

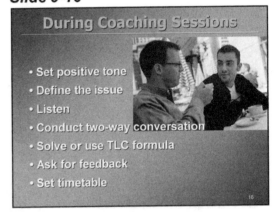

Slide 9-17

Slide 9-18

Slide 9-19

Slide 9-20

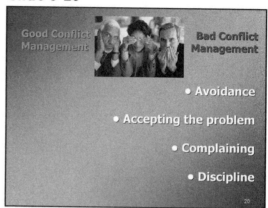

Slide 9-21

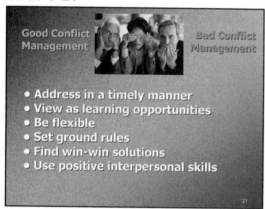

Slide 9-22

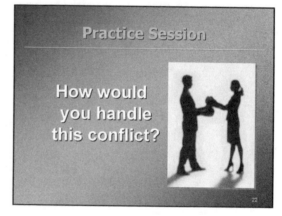

Slide 9-23

Slide 9-24

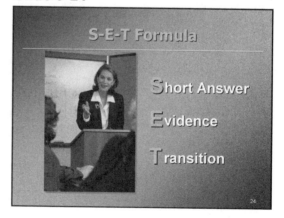

Slide 9-25

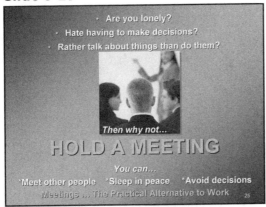

Slide 9-26

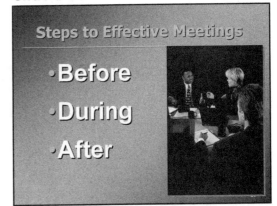

Slide 9-27

Slide 9-28

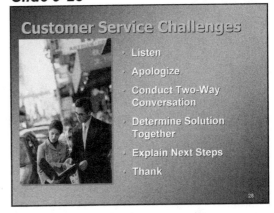

Slide 9-29

Slide 9-30

Slide 9-31

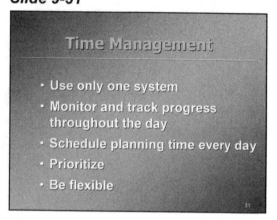

Slide 9-32

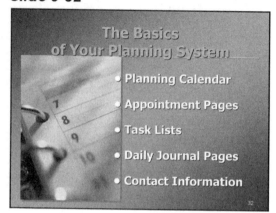

Slide 9-33

Slide 9-34

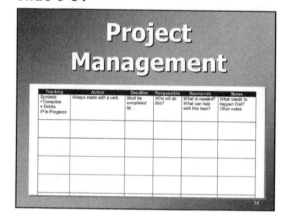

Slide 9-35

Slide 9-36

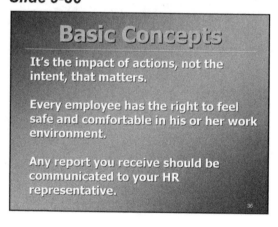

Slide 9-37

Slide 9-38

Slide 9-39

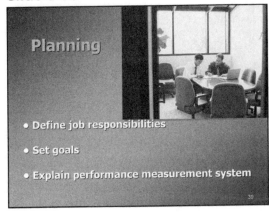

Slide 9-40

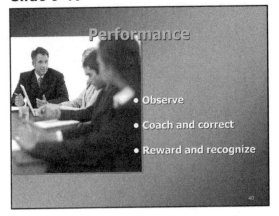

Slide 9-41

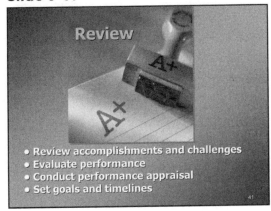

Slide 9-42

Slide 9-43

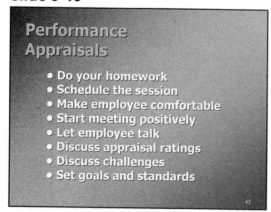

Slide 9-44

Slide 9-45

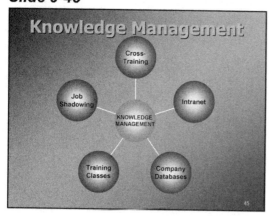

Slide 9-46

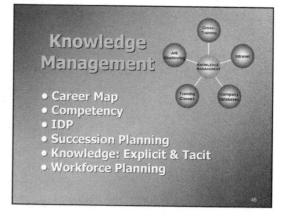

Slide 9-47

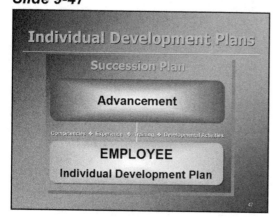

Slide 9-48

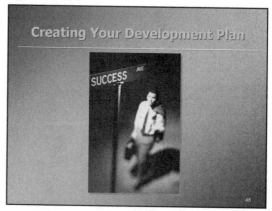

Slide 9-49

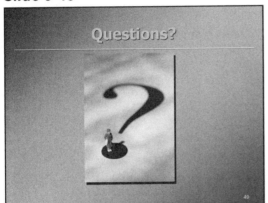

Slide 9-50

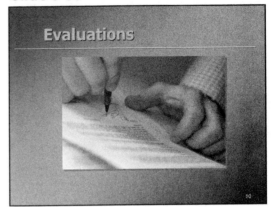

Slide 9-51

◆

Two-Day Program

- ◆ Objectives for the two-day manager skills workshop
- ◆ Lists of materials for facilitator and participants
- ◆ Detailed program agenda to be used as a facilitator's guide

The two-day workshop provides time for learners to first discuss and then practice both interpersonal and functional managerial skills. Day one of the workshop focuses on the interpersonal or soft skills. Day two emphasizes the functional or hard competencies that a manager needs to master. The length of this workshop enables attendees to participate in discussions and then practice the skills that are addressed in each section. At the end of the workshop, learners will create an action plan for continued development.

Training Objectives

The participants' objectives for the two-day manager skills workshop are to be able to

- ◆ apply effective interpersonal skills in the duties of manager
- ◆ apply effective functional skills in the duties of manager
- ◆ adapt skills to accommodate the needs of different situations
- ◆ create an action plan for continued development.

Materials

For the facilitator:

- ◆ this chapter for reference and use as a facilitator guide
- ◆ Learning Activity 11–1: Introductions

- Learning Activity 11–2: The Best Manager I Ever Knew . . .

- Learning Activity 11–3: Interpersonal Skills Practice

- Learning Activity 11–4: Coaching Session Dos and Don'ts

- Learning Activity 11–5: Motivating Employees

- Learning Activity 11–6: Resolving Conflict

- Learning Activity 11–7: Presentation Skills

- Learning Activity 11–8: Effective Meeting Exercise

- Learning Activity 11–9: Customer Service Practice

- Learning Activity 11–10: Business Writing Practice

- Learning Activity 11–11: Q&A Review Session

- Learning Activity 11–12: To Tell the Truth! Review

- Learning Activity 11–13: Time Management Exercise

- Learning Activity 11–14: Project Management Exercise

- Learning Activity 11–15: Decision Charts

- Learning Activity 11–16: Legal Issues

- Learning Activity 11–17: Performance Appraisal Practice

- Learning Activity 11–18: Creating Teams

- Learning Activity 11–19: Problem Solving Activity

- Learning Activity 11–20: Development Plan

- Assessment 12–1: Manager Skills Assessment

- Assessment 12–2: Evaluation Form

- Training Instrument 12–1: The Best Manager I Ever Knew . . .

- Training Instrument 12–2: Interpersonal Skills

- Training Instrument 12–3: Coaching Skills

- Training Instrument 12–4: Motivating Employees

- Training Instrument 12–5: Resolving Conflict

- Training Instrument 12–6: Presentation Skills

- Training Instrument 12–7: Effective Meetings

- Training Instrument 12–8: Customer Service

- Training Instrument 12–9: Business Writing

- Training Instrument 12–10: Time Management

- Training Instrument 12–11: Project Management Chart

- Training Instrument 12–12: Decision Charts

- Training Instrument 12–13: Legal Issues

- Training Instrument 12–14: Performance Appraisals

- Training Instrument 12–15: Creating Teams

- Training Instrument 12–16: Problem Solving

- Training Instrument 12–17: Development Plan

- Tool 12–1: Coaching Steps

- Tool 12–2: Conflict Management Strategies

- Tool 12–3: Presentation Design Form

- Tool 12–4: Agenda Form

- Tool 12–5: Meeting Planning Form

- Tool 12–6: Minutes Format

- Tool 12–7: Brainstorming

- Tool 12–8: Customer Service Formula

- Tool 12–9: Business Writing Tips

- Tool 12–10: Time Management

- Tool 12–11: Project Management

- Tool 12–12: Decision Grid

- Tool 12–13: Decision Chart

- Tool 12–14: Assessment Chart

◆ Tool 12–15: Recordkeeping

◆ Tool 12–16: Performance Management Process

◆ Tool 12–17: Performance Appraisals

◆ Tool 12–18: Problem Solving

◆ Tool 12–19: Knowledge Management

◆ Tool 12–20: Individual Development Plan

◆ PowerPoint slide program, titled "Manager Skills" (slides 10–1 through 10–90). To access slides for this program, open the file *Two-Day.ppt* on the accompanying website. Thumbnail versions of the slides for this two-day workshop are included at the end of this chapter.

◆ projector, screen, and computer for displaying PowerPoint slides; alternatively, overhead transparencies and overhead projector

◆ flipchart and markers

◆ pens or pencils for each participant

◆ name badges for each participant

◆ three-ring binders for each participant

◆ packet of index cards

◆ sticky notes attached to the front of each binder

◆ assorted toys and puzzles for the participant tables

◆ snacks and candy as desired.

First Day

8:00 a.m.   Welcome (5 minutes)

As participants enter the room have slide 10–1 showing on the screen. Welcome them and ask them to use one of the sticky notes on the front of their binders to write one of the main challenges they face as a manager. If they're new managers, they can write about one area that most concerns them. Once they've written their notes, instruct them to go up and attach them to the "What Do I Need From This Workshop?" flipchart page displayed at the front of the room.

Introduce yourself and explain that the purpose of the workshop is to introduce tools and techniques to help them in their roles as managers. If you have experienced managers in the group, this is a good time to note that it's impressive to see managers with varying levels of seniority in this workshop, because that illustrates one of the most important lessons you'll be discussing today: the example that managers set by being willing to continue learning and being open to new ideas. This example helps their employees accept coaching and developmental ideas in a positive light.

Explain the ground rules for the session. Here are some sample ground rules and housekeeping items:

◆ Silence cell phones. (It's a good practice to perform this action on your own cell phone at this time. It demonstrates leading by example and allows you to ensure that your phone isn't the one that rings during the session.)

◆ This workshop is interactive. Be prepared to participate!

◆ There will be scheduled breaks in the morning and afternoon.

◆ Lunch break will be one hour.

◆ Restrooms, smoking areas, snacks, and vending machines are located in the following areas: *[add details]*.

◆ Respectful communication is required. If someone is speaking, all attention should be given to that person.

If participants don't know the area, it's a good idea to have maps to nearby restaurants or menus they can use to order lunch.

8:05   Objectives (5 minutes)

Show slide 10–2. Review the workshop objectives from the slide. The basic understanding should be that a number of subjects will be addressed during the course of this workshop, and they are not expected to be experts in all of them by the end of the two days. This course serves as an overview of tools and techniques that will help them in their continuing development in the subjects addressed.

8:10   Agenda (5 minutes)

Show slide 10–3. Go through the agenda items and ask for any questions.

8:15   What Do I Need From This Workshop? (5 minutes)

Show slide 10–4. Read the sticky notes from the flipchart and assure attendees that the program will address those topics. You'll be able to refer to these as you close each topic to ensure that related questions have been answered. If any of the topics listed aren't discussed, you can add them to the question-and-answer (Q&A) period at the end of the workshop.

8:20   Introductions (15 minutes)

Show slide 10–5. Perform the activity as described in Learning Activity 11–1: Introductions. Once you've completed the activity, refer to the flipchart pages and note that you now have a good starter list of manager's skills to focus on today, but there are many more. Explain that this next activity will allow them to look at other skills that they'll want to develop.

8:35   The Best Manager I Ever Knew . . . (20 minutes)

Show slide 10–6. Distribute Training Instrument 12–1. Perform the activity as described in Learning Activity 11–2: The Best Manager I Ever Knew. This discussion sets the stage for the following assessment of manager skills.

You can transition to this assessment by noting that many of the skills and traits of successful managers are represented in this room. The following assessment will help them discover their strengths and give them some ideas of skills they can develop.

8:55   Self-Assessment (20 minutes)

Show slide 10–7. Distribute Assessment 12–1. Ask learners to complete this assessment individually. Assure them that the answers they give are for their eyes only, so they can be completely candid.

When everyone is finished, briefly discuss the questions on the assessment. Ask if they discovered areas that they would like to develop. Allow volunteers to share some of the areas in which they feel strong. Ask if anyone wants to share areas they have discovered need development, but do not force them to respond. Explain that the materials in today's workshop are designed to help them in each of those areas.

Show slide 10–8. The manager skills on this slide are samples from competency listings used by organizations to assess and develop the skills of their managers.

9:15   The Roles of the Manager . . . (10 minutes)

Show slide 10–9. Ask learners to call out the different activities a manager is called on to perform each day. Use a flipchart to list these. You can get them started by mentioning one or two examples, such as handling payroll or interviewing potential employees.

Once you have a list of activities, ask them to help you sort these into two groups. Use a colored marker to circle the items that use interpersonal skills, often called people skills or soft skills. Note that the rest of the activities deal with tasks, including processes and information systems. These are sometimes referred to as functional, or hard skills. Refer back to the flipchart pages posted around the room with the other manager skills written on them to demonstrate that the same is also true of those lists.

These are the two basic responsibilities of managers— dealing with people and dealing with tasks. Explain that, in this workshop, they'll practice their skills in both of these areas.

9:25   Interpersonal Skills . . . (15 minutes)

Show slide 10–10. Introduce this section by noting that, in the distinction between dealing with people and dealing with tasks, today is the day to concentrate on the people skills, or interpersonal communication techniques. Because many of the roles they discussed dealt with handling emotions, conflict, and change in the workplace, it is essential that managers be able to communicate clearly and effectively. Today will give them an opportunity to determine their level of success with their communication skills and how they can continue to make those skills more effective.

Show slide 10–11: Listening Skills. Remind them that the best communication skill we can practice is the one we can do without saying a word: Listening. But not just any listening will do. It must be active listening. Ask them to compare the kind of listening they do when they listen to television commercials with the kind of listening they do when a doctor is giving them instructions on how to take their medicine. Is it the same? One hopes not.

Active listening is the kind of listening managers need to develop, and it's a hard skill to maintain with all the distractions present in the workplace. Go to the flipchart and write the title: "Active Listening." Ask them for examples of things they do that indicate they are actively listening to someone. To get them started you can mention such activities as nodding, maintaining eye contact, taking notes, ignoring the phone, turning away from the computer, summarizing what they have heard, asking questions, making listening noises, and using body language.

List these ideas on the page as they call them out and ask them to make note of these in the Developmental Activities section of their assessment form, so they can make an effort to incorporate more of them into their daily interactions. Remove this page from the flipchart and post it so that it stays visible throughout the day and you can add other notes or suggestions as they are mentioned.

Show slide 10–12: Communication Skills. Title a flipchart page: "Communications." Discuss the three parts of oral communication: words, tone, and body language. Create a column for each of these on the flipchart page.

Conduct a quick demonstration of how these need to work together by showing a negative example. Cross your arms, look stern, and say angrily, "I really hope you're having a nice day."

Ask what the problem with this communication is. After they have brought up your tone and body language, agree and follow up by noting how often managers send these same kinds of conflicting messages. For example, a manager might say he or she is listening to an employee, but presents a different message if he or she checks email while the employee is talking.

Ask for ways that managers can be more effective with their words, tone, and body language and list them in the appropriate column on the flipchart page, instructing participants to add these to the developmental activities on the assessment form.

Examples of words would include using positive language, appropriate vocabulary, and avoiding acronyms until after you have explained them to the listener.

Examples of tone would include being aware of mood, taking time to calm down so that tone is even and relaxed, speaking at an appropriate volume, avoiding a condescending or sarcastic tone, and being upbeat in communications.

Examples of body language might include maintaining eye contact; smiling; leaning toward the person; and avoiding negative body language such as tapping their feet, looking at their watches, sighing, or grimacing.

Show slide 10–13 and ask for volunteers to summarize this section by reviewing a few ideas of how to be effective with each of the three parts of a message. These could be examples taken from the previous discussion or other ideas they have thought of.

Explain that they will get a chance to practice some of these skills when they return from the 15-minute break.

9:40   Break (15 minutes)

9:55   Interpersonal Skills Practice (40 minutes)

Show slide 10–14. Inform the group that this is an opportunity to apply some of the interpersonal skills they have been discussing. Perform the activity as described in Learning Activity 11–3.

Transition to the next section by reminding learners that, just as they send cues to their listeners through active listening, body language, words, and tone, they are also receiving cues at all times. Observational skills can help them use those cues to discover issues in the workplace before they become major problems.

10:35   Observational Skills (10 minutes)

Show slide 10–15. Title a flipchart page: "Observations." Create two columns. Label one "Behaviors" and the second "Possible Translations." Ask them to think of the kinds of messages that employees send out every day. These could include behaviors such as refusal to do something, reluctance to talk to others, avoidance of certain areas, becoming silent and withdrawn, and nervous tics. List a number of these in the Behaviors column. Now, ask the participants to come up with possible causes for these behaviors. These could include stress, work overload, coworker conflicts, workplace harassment, violence issues, or even problems outside the office.

Remind them that these are the sorts of cues they need to be on the lookout for at all times. Noticing these behaviors can help them discover and address the underlying issues before they become major problems. And how do they address these issues? They use coaching skills like the ones you'll discuss in the next segment of the workshop. Post the Observations flipchart page in the room so the flipchart is cleared and ready for the next topic.

10:45   Coaching Skills (15 minutes)

Show slide 10–16. Note that, if they use the observation skills that you've just discussed, they are going to discover opportunities for coaching and feedback. Additionally, there are many other times they'll need to use coaching skills. Title a flipchart page: "Coaching Opportunities." Ask for examples of times when they'll need to coach, teach, or counsel employees. Among the answers you can offer to get them started are

- ◆ when a person is new to a position
- ◆ when a person takes on new duties
- ◆ when someone is going on vacation and needs a backup
- ◆ when someone is showing signs of frustration
- ◆ when mistakes are made
- ◆ when an employee is procrastinating because he or she doesn't know how to do something
- ◆ when the employee asks for help.

These are just a few of the times when coaching and feedback may be necessary. Remind them that they don't have to wait for a problem to appear to coach employees. Coaching individuals to help in their growth and development is an important responsibility of a manager and ensures that employees do not equate all coaching sessions with negative feedback.

To make the most of these coaching opportunities, suggest that managers make use of the guidelines for effective coaching. You can solicit their ideas on each of these actions and summarize with the notes for before, during, and after a coaching session.

Show slide 10–17. These are the things a manager should do before a coaching session.

- ◆ Observe—Often called MBWA (managing by walking around), this is the best way for a manager to stay in touch with what is going on in his or her department. If problems or areas for development are observed, this gives the manager an opportunity to look into these before they become major issues.

- ◆ Schedule time for coaching—Although many coaching sessions can be impromptu and informal events, major coaching sessions should be scheduled so that time is available to adequately address the subject. Coaching sessions should not be rushed events.

- ◆ Prepare for coaching discussions—Managers should do their homework before coaching sessions. If it is a corrective-action session, the manager needs to have done research and gathered specific information on the situation.

Show slide 10–18. These are the actions a manager can take to conduct an effective coaching session.

- Set a positive tone—The coaching session may be about a negative experience, but it does not have to take a negative tone. Starting the session by stating the positive outcomes that are expected and even noting the employee's strengths in other areas can be ways to ensure that the person is not immediately put on the defensive.

- Define the issue—Clearly and objectively stating the issue to be discussed is important so that misunderstandings do not occur.

- Listen—The most important thing a manager can do in a coaching session may be to listen. An employee might need to vent, explain, or confirm that he or she understands the topic that is being addressed. Allowing the employee to vent is an effective way to get past the emotions that may prohibit progress, as long as it does not go on for too long and turn into a "gripe session."

- Conduct two-way communication—A coaching conversation can become negative quickly if a person feels he or she is being lectured to. Explaining the situation and its consequences to the workplace is vital, just as allowing input from the person is necessary to ensure the open exchange of information.

- Determine the solution (if the session is corrective feedback)—Allow the person to give ideas first. Giving him or her the chance to have input will help the employee accept the resolution to the situation.

- Use the TLC process of training (if the session is developmental)—Teach the process or information. Listen as employees explain or demonstrate their understanding of the process. Coach them on any adjustments they need to make.

◆ Ask for feedback—Ask how they feel about the solution reached or the process they have learned. Allow them to ask questions.

◆ Set a timetable for follow-up—Decide when you will get back together to revisit this coaching topic.

Show slide 10–19. These are the steps a manager will want to take following a coaching session.

◆ Follow up—Meet as scheduled to review the process, make additional adjustments, address continuing issues, or move to the next level of development.

◆ Recognize accomplishments—This is an excellent opportunity to recognize the development of this employee. Use reward and recognition practices if appropriate.

11:00   Coaching Skills Practice (20 minutes)

Show slide 10–20. Distribute Tool 12–1 and perform the activity as described in Learning Activity 11–4: Coaching Session Dos and Don'ts.

Remind them that the effective use of these coaching techniques, along with motivational strategies, will cultivate a positive atmosphere in their workplaces. Those motivational strategies are what you'll discuss next.

11:20   Motivating Employees (10 minutes)

Show slide 10–21. Ask what they think motivates employees. Use a flipchart page to list their ideas. Once you have assembled a list of items, explain to them that numerous surveys have been done on this subject. And, although some items bounce around on the list, the top five motivators are usually the same. Click each item on the PowerPoint presentation until you get to the number-one motivator.

And the survey says that employees are motivated by

    5. money

    4. job security

    3. a feeling of inclusion (teamwork, input, opportunities)

    2. recognition for a job well done

    1. challenges (goals, risks, change, learning).

The top motivator, challenges, is all about learning new skills, trying new activities, and achieving goals. This usually surprises people because most people automatically think money is the main motivator.

If they disagree, it's fun to ask, "How many of you could be making more money doing what you're doing somewhere else?" With most groups, especially governmental agencies or associations, you'll find a large number who will raise their hands. You can then point out that obviously money wasn't their main motivation in choosing this position. Participants often join in the conversation by saying what they like about their company.

This is an excellent way to illustrate that not everyone is motivated solely by money in their choice of careers or positions. That's why the motivators we offer as employee incentives and rewards don't always take the form of cash. And, in organizations in which cash bonuses are not an option, these other motivators are even more important.

Keeping this in mind, you're going to give them an opportunity to share best practices for motivating employees that they have used or heard about.

11:30   Motivating Employees Activity (20 minutes)

Show slide 10–22. Divide the group into four new teams to allow them to work with a new group of participants. Perform the activity as described in Learning Activity 11–5: Motivating Employees.

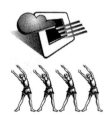

Summarize this topic by noting that, even with our best coaching skills and motivators, it is inevitable that there will be some conflict in a workplace. That's the next subject you'll cover.

11:50   Resolving Conflict (10 minutes)

Show slide 10–23. Start this section by telling the group that conflict in the workplace can be a good thing. Conflict is a natural result of a diverse thinking, and it is this thinking that makes us question the status quo, consider new ideas, and develop innovative ways of improving outdated processes. It's when conflict is ignored, stifled, or allowed to escalate that problems arise.

Distribute Tool 12–2. Show slide 10–24. Compare the differences between good and bad conflict management, asking for their input as you discuss these points.

Bad conflict management includes avoiding conflict altogether. Ask them why this is the case. You might discuss how new ideas are never heard if the dominant people are never questioned. This lowers morale and can create a stagnant team.

Other conflict management issues include accepting the problem, or complaining rather than addressing the problem. This creates a negative atmosphere and they might find that other unrelated situations begin to be blamed on the conflict, as it becomes a scapegoat for the real issues that need to be addressed.

A final conflict management technique that is not always a good idea is discipline. Disciplining the team or taking punitive action may not address the actual reason the conflict exists and may increase divisive feelings among members of the team.

Show slide 10–25. Explain that good conflict management practices include addressing the conflicts in a timely manner and classifying them as learning opportunities. Even personality conflicts can teach you about how different team members operate and can help individuals learn to understand each other better.

Other good techniques include being flexible and creative in resolutions, setting ground rules so that all ideas can be shared without being criticized, and looking for win–win resolutions. Interpersonal skills such as listening, using appropriate body language and tone, asking questions, using positive language, avoiding distractions, and resisting the urge to interrupt will also help in resolving conflict situations.

Ask for their input on best practices that they have used in these types of situations.

Distribute Training Instrument 12–5. Ask the group to review this situation and help you brainstorm ways to resolve this conflict. Remind them that a rule of brain-storming is that there is no judging of ideas. The goal is to list as many ideas as possible, concentrating on quantity, not quality.

Using a flipchart, list all the ideas presented. Once you have exhausted the list of ideas, discuss some of your favorite ideas from the list. Then, allow the group to choose their favorite ideas by a show of hands.

12:00   Lunch (60 minutes)

1:00   Resolving Conflict Activity (25 minutes)

Show slide 10–26. Perform the activity as described in Learning Activity 11–6: Resolving Conflict.

Remind them that, as you have discovered earlier today, miscommunication can come from conflicting interpersonal skills. An important interpersonal skill is our ability to communicate information clearly and in a positive manner. The next section will help develop that skill, whether they are presenting that information to one person or to a large audience.

1:25   Presentation Skills (15 minutes)

Show slide 10–27. Note that the parts of a presentation include the introduction, the main points, and the conclusion. Distribute Tool 12–3. They will be able to use this format to create presentations. You can briefly walk them through this form by referring to the instructions in each section.

Continue by reminding them that an important component of effective presentation skills is the ability to condense a message into the least possible amount of time. Quite often they will have a limited time period to get information across, and organizing their thoughts in advance can help them make more effective use of the time available.

Show slide 10–28. The SET formula is used to get the answer to a question across in the shortest time available, such as the period of an average elevator ride. That's why it's often called "an elevator speech." SET stands for the Short answer, Evidence supporting that short answer, and the Transition, which includes a summary statement and handing the floor back to another person.

Demonstrate an example of this such as this quick answer to the question, "What is an elevator speech?" "An elevator speech is a talk that can be given in 30 to 60 seconds, which is the time span of an average elevator ride. It uses the SET formula of Short answer, Evidence supporting the short answer, and Transition or summary statement. It allows you to give a complete presentation in a limited amount of time. Any questions?"

1:40   Presentation Skills Exercise (25 minutes)

Show slide 10–29. Perform activity as described in Learning Activity 11–7: Presentation Skills. This exercise not only allows the participants to practice condensing their messages and presenting them, but also gives a review of the information covered in the morning session.

If this has been determined as an area of specific focus for the group, use the full 40-minute version of the exercise and adjust later activities. Otherwise, shorten the time required by instructing learners to present their elevator speeches to the others at their tables, but not to the entire class.

2:05   Break (15 minutes)

2:20   Effective Meetings (15 minutes)

Show slide 10–30. Allow them to read this humorous introduction to the topic of meetings. Ask them if this describes many of the meetings they attend. According to recent statistics, approximately 11 million meetings are held in the United States every day. That translates to about 37 percent of employee time being spent in meetings, according to the National Statistics Council. Additionally, researchers have found that 91 percent of meeting attendees admit to daydreaming during meetings, whereas 39 percent have actually dozed off.

Explain that the time wasted in meetings translates into a loss of money. Show slide 10–31 and explain that this formula determines how much a meeting costs. If you'd like, you can ask someone with a calculator to help you make a quick calculation of the cost of today's session. If you do this activity, estimate salary at about $20 per hour to avoid discussion of salary levels.

Note that the way to make meetings an investment instead of a waste is to prepare for them in advance. The most important steps employees can take to conduct a successful meeting happen before anyone steps foot into the room.

Show slide 10–32. Explain that there are actions they need to take before, during, and afterward to ensure they host an effective meeting. Ask what they think are the necessary steps to take before the meeting. You can note that determining the invitees, creating the agenda, sending out communications, gathering background information, and planning the room layout can all help to make a meeting successful.

The steps that occur during the meeting include posting the agenda, starting on time, using positive facilitation techniques, soliciting participation, and taking complete minutes.

After a meeting, evaluation is useful to determine what worked and what didn't. Also, sending out the minutes and action items with deadlines will remind attendees of what their next steps should be.

Distribute Tools 12–4, 12–5, and 12–6; briefly discuss the instructions given in each section of the tools.

2:35   Effective Meetings Practice (20 minutes)

Show slide 10–33. Break the participants up into three groups. Perform the activity as described in Learning Activity 11–8: Effective Meeting Exercise.

Note that the most effective use of meetings is to bring minds together to come up with ideas and solutions that are better than any single mind could develop. The next segment of the workshop will help develop the right framework for that type of collaborative effort.

2:55   Encouraging Innovation and Creativity (15 minutes)

Show slide 10–34. Remind them that when you have a group gathered for a meeting, you can benefit from their diverse ideas and ways of thinking. If they're not going to do that, they've squandered a valuable opportunity.

Brainstorming is the best way to make use of those minds and that creativity, as long as the rules are followed. Too often people hold meetings and ask for ideas, then immediately critique those ideas as soon as they are proposed. That's a sure way to squash innovative thinking.

Show slide 10–35. Distribute Tool 12–7. Review these basic rules of brainstorming. The goal is quantity of ideas, not quality. The quality work comes later when you start narrowing the idea list. To begin with, you want as many ideas as possible. No judging of ideas is allowed during brainstorming. So, no one is allowed to say, "That won't work" or "We don't have the budget for that." And piggybacking is allowed. That means that anyone can add their ideas onto other ideas that have been suggested.

Show them this concept in action by choosing one topic from the "What Do I Need From This Workshop?" flipchart page you posted earlier. Using a new flipchart page, ask them to think of ideas that would help with this challenge and list all suggestions on the page, leaving space in front of each idea.

Invite all the participants to come forward with one of the colored markers from their tables. (If you have colored stickers, they can be used instead of markers.) Explain that this is a simple method used to conduct an informal brainstorming session to select the top ideas. Ask everyone to come forward and put a check in the space in front of their three favorite ideas on the list. Show them how this creates a ranking of the ideas. They would follow up this step by taking the top idea and creating an action plan.

Transition to the next section by noting that they might have to use even more creativity and innovation to resolve some customer situations they may encounter as a manager. That's what the next section will address.

3:10   Customer Service Basics (15 minutes)

Show slide 10–36. Note that when a manager is called in, it usually means that a customer service situation has hit a snag. The formula you're reviewing with them is a reminder of the basic steps of resolving customer challenges.

Show slide 10–37. Distribute Tool 12–8. Discuss the steps of resolving customer challenges, including:

- Listen—Sometimes a person just wants to know that his or her concern has been heard. Allowing the customer to vent can help reduce tension and set the stage for resolution.

- Apologize—This doesn't mean accepting blame. This simply means apologizing for the customer having had a negative experience.

- Conduct a two-way conversation—This means asking questions, discussing, and listening as you try to get to the root of the situation so that you can determine what the actual problem is that you are trying to resolve.

- Determine solution together—Allow the customer to offer his or her possible solutions first. Note that often the customer actually has a less drastic resolution than the one the manager may be thinking of. And of course, they never want to tell the customer what *can't* be done. Instead the response should be reworded to express what *can* be done.

- Explain what will happen next—Let the customer know exactly what steps will occur and the timeline needed for these steps to be put into action.

- Thank them—Employees will want to end the conversation by thanking the customer for calling their attention to this situation and allowing them to be able to solve it instead of leaving the customer unhappy.

3:25   Customer Challenge Practice (25 minutes)

Show slide 10–38. Perform the activity as explained in Learning Activity 11–9: Customer Challenge Practice.

For the next communications topic, explain that you want to move from the spoken word to the written word.

3:50   Business Writing (10 minutes)

Show slide 10–39. Introduce this section by noting that, in many businesses, customers never step foot inside the building. A large proportion of that business is conducted on the phone, but an increasing number of transactions are being performed through written communications via email and online locations. Share an example in which you've read something in an email that misrepresented its intended purpose, used negative wording, or had obvious errors. Ask them if they have had similar experiences. Ask them how those errors affected their image of that company and the person sending the message.

That's why it's so important for managers to be aware of the accuracy and tone of their written communications, whether it's an internal email or memo, or public communications such as reports or press releases. Show slide 10–40 and review the tips listed for business writing. Remind them that they should always perform spelling and grammar checks through their computer program to avoid possible embarrassment.

Show slide 10–41 and review the additional tips for business writing. Distribute Tool 12–9. These are guidelines to create effective written communications.

4:00   Business Writing Exercise (15 minutes)

Show slide 10–42. Perform the activity as described in Learning Activity 11–10: Business Writing Practice. Adjust the time by deleting step five of the activity so that participants present only to the others in their groups. However, if the class is running ahead of time at this point, you can include those full class presentations.

After they have completed this exercise, congratulate the participants on their performance for the day and tell them that now you'd like to be sure they got what they needed from today's session.

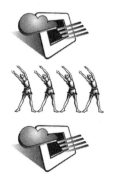

4:15   Question-and-Answer Session (25 minutes)

Show slide 10–43. Perform the activity as described in Learning Activity 11–11: Q&A Review Session.

Show slide 10–44. End the activity by opening the floor to questions and checking your flipchart page from the beginning of the class for additional questions. Don't worry if you can't answer all of the questions. There's always something that catches us unaware in these sessions! If it's something you'll need to research or it's a topic that will be covered in the second day of the course, tell them you'll have the information for them at the next session.

Remind them that one way we show that we are leaders is by exhibiting a readiness to accept ideas for improvement. So, now you'd like their ideas for improvement by having them fill out an evaluation form.

4:40   Evaluations (5 minutes)

Show slide 10–45. Distribute Assessment 12–2 and ask them to take a few minutes to complete this form so that you can make adjustments to the class that can make day two even more productive for them.

Show slide 10–46. Confirm the time, date, and location of the second day of the workshop.

Thank them for their attention and end with a motivating story, quote, or anecdote from your collection.

4:45   Adjourn

Second Day

8:00 a.m.   Welcome (5 minutes)

As participants enter the training room, have slide 10–47 showing on the screen. Invite them to be seated, show slide 10–48, and run through the day's agenda. Have a copy of this agenda posted on a flipchart page where everyone can see it throughout the day.

Tell them that you know that many of them have issues going on back at their workplaces that they are concerned about right now. Explain that this next activity is designed to help them put those problems aside for the day.

8:05   Leave Your Problems at the Door Activity (10 minutes)

Show slide 10–49. Ask them to think of a challenge that is waiting for them back at the office. They should write down this issue and a description of its main considerations on a piece of paper. Tell them to be sure that they list enough details so that someone else could look at the problem and suggest possible solutions. If they have difficulty thinking of challenges, you can get them started by giving them ideas such as an employee with a negative attitude, a person who doesn't seem to be able to learn a process, someone who is not challenged enough in his or her work, or a potential harassment situation.

Once they have written down their challenges, walk around the room and collect them in a box or a hat. Remind them that now they have left their office problems behind and you hope this will help them focus on getting the most out of today's workshop. Also tell them that they'll be getting some help on this problem before the day is over.

8:15   To Tell the Truth! (15 minutes)

Show slide 10–50. Perform the activity as described in Learning Activity 11–12: To Tell the Truth!

This exercise starts this second session with an interactive review of items from the first session. If there have been multiple days since the first session, you can add to this review by asking learners if they have used any of the tools from the first workshop. You can give bonus "eye-openers" such as candy to those who contribute to the discussion to encourage early morning responses.

8:30   Manager Competencies (10 minutes)

Show slide 10–51. Ask learners to refer to the assessment they completed in the previous class. Remind them that in the previous class they worked with interpersonal skills. Today's session focuses on tasks and processes.

Ask if their assessment revealed functional skills that they would like to develop. Allow volunteers to share some of the areas in which they feel they excel. Ask if anyone wants to share areas for development that they have discovered. Explain that the materials in today's workshop are designed to help them in each of those areas.

Show slide 10–52. They may remember from the previous class that the skills on this chart are from sample competency listings used by organizations to assess and develop the skills of their managers. Ask which ones they see as functional competencies, or skills that deal with tasks and processes. Three of these—resource management, results orientation, and strategic thinking—deal with functional skills. Those are included in the group of skills that will be addressed during today's workshop.

8:40   Time Management Concepts (20 minutes)

Show slide 10–53. Introduce this section to participants by explaining that you'd like to start this discussion on time management by looking at how they manage their days. Ask for a show of hands of how many attendees use a planning system every day. Ask how many of them feel that their system of choice is effective in the management of their time. If not, assure them that they're not alone. There's a reason that so many time management systems, software packages, books, and classes exist today. We all have challenges in managing the events and tasks of our lives.

Write on a flipchart: "Time Wasters." Ask them what their biggest challenges to staying on schedule are. You'll get a variety of answers including the phone, email, people interrupting them, and crises. Acknowledge that all of these are a part of the job of manager. Without those interruptions, organizations might not even need managers! But by using a few select tools and guidelines, they will be able to more effectively manage both the interruptions and the scheduling of their time.

Show slide 10–54. Distribute Tool 12–10. These are the basics of any time management system.

- ◆ Use only one system. Ask how many of them use multiple systems, such as Outlook, a PDA, a cellphone organizer, a notebook, or even the refrigerator door at home to track different events and activities. Ask if they can see what the problem might be with this planning method. The answer is that there's only one of each of them and there's only one 5:00 p.m. each day. So, if they have their child's soccer game listed on the refrigerator door at home and they're still at work at 5:00 p.m., what's going to happen? Right. They now have an angry child. Keeping all appointments, professional and private, in one location eliminates this possibility. If they're uncomfortable with having their private appointments listed in this book, suggest they create their own codes for them.

- ◆ Monitor and track progress throughout the day. This means checking off items as they are completed, making note of start and stop times of activities, and even making notes of interruptions. This will not only help them analyze the areas where they need to make adjustments, but will help them when they return from an interruption, because they can look at their notes to see what they were working on before they were called away.

◆ Schedule planning time every day. It might be in the morning before anyone else gets into the office. It might be in the evening as they review their accomplishments for the day. No matter what the time, this session should include a review of the day's tasks to see which were completed or deleted, and scheduling of those that need to be completed on another day.

◆ Prioritize. Left to our own devices, many of us have a tendency to do the easy tasks first and keep putting off the more involved activities. Instead, remind them that they need to use the daily planning session to prioritize and determine the most important activities and those with impending deadlines. Scheduling those first will ensure they meet goals, and the smaller tasks can be scheduled around the more important ones.

◆ Be flexible. Remind them that interruptions will still occur. Firefighting will still be necessary. But advance planning will help them ensure that when they get back from firefighting, they're ready to jump right back in on the highest priority task on their list.

Show slide 10–55 and review the forms for scheduling and tracking daily activities. It's important to note that it doesn't matter what system they're using. It just needs to work for them. Some basics that they want to be sure are included in their system are listed on this slide.

They need a planning calendar, so they can look at a glance to see what days are open. Since this calendar only has space blocked out with a general description of the event, they also need daily or weekly appointment pages to list details of those engagements. They need notes pages, either daily or weekly, to allow them to record all of their daily activities, meeting notes, and phone call information.

Other items are not as essential. Phone and contact lists are often kept on our phones or in our email databases, so having them in their planners can be optional for them. Sections for specific ongoing projects or clients can be useful if they will have numerous meetings and would like to keep all the information in one place. They can make their planner system as simple or elaborate as they wish. Once again, the main point is that they have to use it consistently to make it work for them.

9:00   Time Management Exercise (20 minutes)

Show slide 10–56. Perform the activity as described in Learning Activity 11–13: Time Management Exercise.

When you have completed the activity, remind them that a natural extension of managing time is the need to manage the time and projects of teams. Project management is the next topic you'll be focusing on.

9:20   Managing Projects (15 minutes)

Show slide 10–57. Explain to them that project management includes the same principles as time management, with the added dimension of having more than one person to get the tasks done.

Show slide 10–58. Distribute Tool 12–11. Review the chart with them to illustrate the basic concepts of project management.

The chart is simply populated with all the items that need to be completed for the project. But, because a task list without accountability or deadlines is going to be a task list that won't get completed, they'll want to use all the additional columns recommended on this chart.

The tasks are created by brainstorming and then compiled into a list. The list is reviewed to determine the order in which tasks need to be completed. Then, they determine who will take ownership of each task, decide on deadlines, and assemble a list of resources that can help with the tasks.

By posting this chart, either physically in the office or on a shared database, the manager can keep the team's attention focused on the next steps of the project and offer a visual reminder to those who have deadlines coming up.

You can also note that other options to track these tasks include various project management software programs or even using Microsoft Excel to create a simple version of a project management system.

The best way to understand the concept of project management is to jump in and experience it. That's what the next exercise will allow them to do.

9:35   Project Management Exercise (20 minutes)

Show slide 10–59. Perform the activity as described in Learning Activity 11–14: Project Management Exercise. Adjust the length to 20 minutes by eliminating group presentations.

Transition to the next section by explaining that, once a project is underway, there will be decisions to be made and this is an area that many managers find challenging. Wanting to be open-minded and listening to all views and suggestions, managers sometimes find themselves encountering "paralysis by analysis." The next section will look at some logical systems to help them make decisions with their teams or for their departments.

9:55   Break (15 minutes)

10:10   Decision Making (15 minutes)

Show slide 10–60. Introduce this section by noting that there are numerous methods that can be used to weigh the pros and cons of any decision, and there is no substitute for conducting research, consulting resources, benchmarking the best practices of others, and drawing on personal experience to assess the information needed to make decisions. What you will focus on now are some of the tools that allow managers to compare all of this input and make an informed choice.

Show slide 10–61. Distribute Tools 12–12, 12–13, and 12–14. Explain that the Decision Grid is useful for organizing priorities for departmental projects. Consult the instructions to explain how the grid works.

The Brainstorming Grid is another simple tool used to rank ideas from a brainstorming session or a committee meeting. It can also be used as a tool when assessing applicants for a position. Walk through the instructions on these tools and ask them if they can think of any other potential uses for them.

10:25   Decision-Making Practice (20 minutes)

Show slide 10–62. Perform the activity as described in Learning Activity 11–15: Decision Charts.

10:45   Managing Records (15 minutes)

Show slide 10–63. Introduce this subject by explaining that managing tasks is important, but equally important are the tools they use to complete and monitor those tasks.

Show slide 10–64. Distribute Tool 12–15. This tool has guidelines to help them design their record systems for maximum efficiency. Discuss the guidelines and solicit additional best practices from the group.

Transition to the next segment by recognizing that all of the documentation they are maintaining may sometimes seem excessive, but it's essential to have in the event of the next topic you'll be discussing: legal issues.

11:00   Legal Issues (25 minutes)

Show slide 10–65. Perform the activity as described in Learning Activity 11–16: Legal Issues. Allow time for discussion. Don't be surprised if questions come up in this section that you can't answer. Laws change, interpretations are different, and there are many variations based on your location. And you never want to try to guess when it comes to legal issues! Just make a list of any questions that you weren't sure about so you can research them and email the group with answers later.

Summarize the legal discussion by showing slide 10–66 and reviewing a few basics.

- ◆ Explain that it's the effect of their actions, not the intent, that matters.

- ◆ Legal issues that are brought to them should never be handled carelessly or with disregard.

- ◆ Not only the company, but the manager, can be held liable in legal complaints.

- ◆ The employee has a right to a safe, comfortable working environment. A manager should be aware of potential problems and address them in a timely manner.

- ◆ Laws change and new precedents are being set every day. If they have the slightest doubt about an employee issue, they should talk to their human resources representative.

11:25   Performance Management (20 minutes)

Show slide 10–67. Explain that the next segment will address the stages of performance management. Distribute Tool 12–16 and discuss these main phases of the performance management cycle.

Show slide 10–68 and explain the cycle of performance management.

Performance management starts with the planning stage during which the manager works with the employee to prepare him or her for the work that will be performed. The performance stage is the actual performance of the work and coaching for improvement throughout the year. The review stage is looking back to evaluate the year's accomplishments and challenges. And then the cycle begins again.

Explain that you'd like to study each of these stages in more detail.

◆ Show slide 10–69. Planning—During this stage they will work with their employees to ensure the employees understand their job responsibilities, their goals, and how their job performance will be measured. To do this, employees will review job descriptions with their department members, create a development plan with goals and timelines, and review the performance appraisal form with employees.

◆ Show slide 10–70. Performance—During this stage, managers are expected to observe operations, conduct coaching sessions with their employees on both a formal and informal basis, and address and guide the correction of performance problems. During this period the manager should also take the time to recognize and reward achievements.

◆ Show slide 10–71. Review—In the final stage of performance management, managers review the accomplishments and challenges of employees, evaluate the performance of each employee, schedule and conduct individual performance appraisal sessions, and set goals and timelines for the upcoming performance period. And with this, the cycle starts over again.

Show slide 10–72 and summarize the cycle to reinforce the information in learners' minds and ask if there are any questions.

Transition to the next section by explaining that, for many managers and employees, their least favorite aspect of performance management is the annual performance appraisal. That is the next section you'll discuss.

Before you break for lunch, remind them of the exact time you need them back in their seats. On the second day of a workshop, you'll often find that participants have become more comfortable and therefore might be a little more lax in their attention to the class guidelines.

11:45   Lunch (60 minutes)

12:45   Appraisals (20 minutes)

Show Slide 10–73. Explain that the final step of performance management is the annual performance appraisal. This step is often dreaded, postponed, or rushed through by managers. It's not a comfortable activity for most managers, but the good news is it can actually be a positive experience if prepared and conducted with the employee's development in mind.

Show slide 10–74. Distribute Tool 12–17. Review these basic considerations of a performance appraisal with the group, allowing comments and personal experiences to be shared.

Explain that they'll now have a chance to conduct a performance appraisal to get a feel for how these suggestions can be implemented.

1:05   Appraisal Practice (45 minutes)

Show slide 10–75. Perform the activity as described in Learning Activity 11–17: Performance Appraisal Practice.

Transition to the next section by reminding them that it is not only the performance of the individual, but also the performance of groups of individuals working together that is vital to their department's goals. The next section will focus on getting those diverse personalities working in unison to achieve desired outcomes.

1:50   Creating Teams (15 minutes)

Show slide 10–76. Remind them of the importance of teams in the workplace, because teams make use of various ideas and differing ways of thinking. They allow workers to learn from each other. And they are a wonderful opportunity for team members to participate in cross-training and to better understand and appreciate the roles of others in the department.

Show slide 10–77 and review the components of effective teams.

The components that make teams effective include

- Challenges—Ask them to think back on that main motivator for employees. Do they see how this could also be a motivator for teams? Without a goal to accomplish, a team has no reason for continuation. Challenges are what make teams compete, excel, and learn.

- Following Team Ground Rules—Setting rules, having boundaries, keeping current with deadlines, and being accountable are all common elements of effective teams. Ask if they have any other ground rules for their teams.

- Opportunities for Performance and Learning— Allowing team members to grow through delegation of projects that require them to learn new processes and information makes team membership a mutually beneficial experience. The team benefits from productivity. The team member grows in experience and expands his or her skills résumé.

- ◆ Diversity—A variety of backgrounds, experiences, and skills allows a team to be stronger than any single member. It ensures that the group doesn't fall back on the concept of "we've always done it that way" because of the different outlooks that bring new ideas to the table. And different personality types also bring valuable insights to the group also. That's the focus on the next activity for developing effective teams.

2:05   Teamwork Activity (35 minutes)

Show slide 10–78. Perform the activity as described in Learning Activity 11–18: Creating Teams.

Follow up this activity by explaining that these teams can be great think-tanks for problem solving and that's just what their team will have an opportunity to do when they return from the break.

2:40   Break (15 minutes)

2:55   Problem Solving (15 minutes)

Show slide 10–79. Explain to the group that this is an opportunity for them to put all of the techniques they've discussed in this workshop into action by solving a real problem. In fact, they're going to solve a problem for someone else in this room.

Pull out the box containing the problems that everyone "left at the door." Instruct each person to take one problem out of the box. Let them look at it to be sure they didn't get their own problem. If they did, they can put it back in and select another.

Show slide 10–80. Distribute Tool 12–18. Review the basics of problem solving.

- ◆ Define the problem—They'll want to determine what the real problem is, which often means digging deeper than their initial impressions.

◆ Analyze the problem—In this stage, they'll conduct research to find the latest information available on the problem.

◆ Consider alternatives—This is the stage where, using best practices, benchmarking, and research, they'll select a number of potential solutions.

◆ Select a solution—Using a decision-making chart or other comparison tools, they'll compare pros and cons to select the solution to implement.

◆ Implement the solution—The solution is broken down into steps using SMART (specific, measurable, achievable, relevant, and time-bound) goals and put into action.

◆ Evaluate—Every problem-solving effort should be evaluated to determine if the solution reached has addressed the original problem, if other solutions should be considered, and to learn from the process so that future problem-solving is more efficient because of the lessons learned.

3:10   Problem Solving Practice (30 minutes)

Show slide 10–81. Perform the activity as described in Learning Activity 11–19: Problem Solving Activity.

Successful problem solving is one of the types of knowledge that helps a company grow. Building on the history of what has worked can help make future efforts more successful. Knowledge management, the next section, will help them build on that history.

3:40   Knowledge Management (15 minutes)

Show slide 10–82. Introduce this segment by asking if there has ever been a time that a process has had to be postponed because the person in the office who normally handled that procedure was out. Ask what effect this had on the department's productivity.

Show slide 10–83. Distribute Tool 12–19. Explain that knowledge management seeks to eliminate problems such as department stalls due to absent employees and the loss of knowledge that occurs when a long-time employee retires. Knowledge management consists of the range of practices that businesses use to identify and share knowledge across the organization. These include practices such as cross-training, job shadowing, training classes, intranet resources, and company databases.

Show slide 10–84. Give a basic overview of knowledge management and how it can benefit their workplaces by explaining the following concepts:

♦ Career Path or Career Map: A predefined set of jobs or positions through which an employee might progress to achieve a desired level in the organization.

♦ Competency: The knowledge, skills, abilities (KSAs) and behaviors that contribute to successful performance in a particular position or occupational level.

♦ Individual Development Plan (IDP): A document that includes an assessment of an employee's current skills and an outline of how the employee will develop the knowledge, skills, and abilities to meet the changing needs of the organization and to achieve future career goals.

♦ Succession Planning: A process designed to create talent pools and learning opportunities to ensure that potential successors are identified and developed to fill key roles in the organization.

♦ Types of Organizational Knowledge: Explicit knowledge is knowledge of company procedures and processes that can be tracked in manuals, directories, and other references. Tacit knowledge is estimated to make up 80 to 85 percent of an organization's knowledge assets. It's composed of people's insight, judgment, and know-how, which requires more interpersonal training methods, such as coaching and mentoring.

- ◆ Workforce Planning: The process of analyzing the current workforce, identifying future workforce needs, and developing solutions to address the gaps that exist between those two.

Show slide 10–85 and explain how an individual development plan is an excellent tool for both their employees and themselves. It helps the manager know what areas an employee needs to develop and what actions are being taken to manifest that growth. It helps employees know what areas will help in their career development and guides their developmental efforts so they are focused on the right activities for their goals.

You can transition to the next segment by noting that now you'd like to give them the opportunity to develop their career paths and IDPs.

3:55   Continued Development Action Plan (20 minutes)

Show slide 10–86. Distribute Tool 12–20. Inform learners that they are now ready for the most important part of any workshop. That part is determining how they will use the information they have received once they have returned to their positions as managers.

Show slide 10–87. Perform the activity as listed in Learning Activity 11–20: Development Plan.

4:15   Q&A (15 minutes)

Show slide 10–88. Open the floor to questions. Also, take this opportunity to look at the sticky notes from the beginning of the session to ensure that all their challenges have been addressed. Don't worry if you can't answer all of the questions. There's always something that catches us unaware in these sessions! If you don't know, tell them you'll find out and get back in touch with them. If everyone wants to know the information, you can send a follow-up email to the entire group and include reminders from the session. It's a great way to keep the workshop information fresh in their minds.

4:30   Evaluations (10 minutes)

Show slide 10–89. Remind them that, just like they are doing with their managerial skills, you want to continue developing your presentation skills. So, now you'd like their ideas for improvement through their comments on the final evaluation form. Distribute Assessment 12–2 and ask them to complete these before they leave.

Show slide 10–90. Thank them for their attention and end with a motivating story, quote, or anecdote from your collection.

4:40   Adjourn

What to Do Next

◆ Using the material in chapter 4 as a guide, build a detailed plan to prepare for this workshop.

◆ Schedule a training room and invite your attendees.

◆ Draft a supply list, teaching notes, and time estimates.

◆ Decide how you will support the action plan to which your learners will commit.

◆ Evaluate the effectiveness of the program, using ideas from chapter 6.

◆ Consider designing follow-up sessions to encourage the learners to continue developing manager skills.

Slide 10-1

Slide 10-2

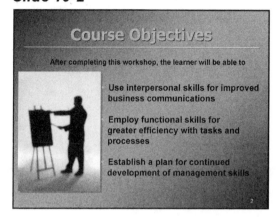

Slide 10-3

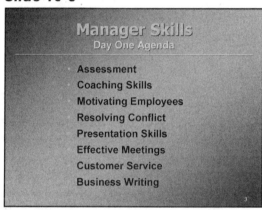

Slide 10-4

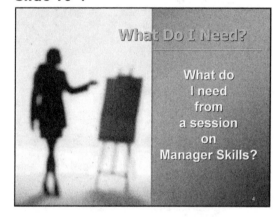

Slide 10-5

Slide 10-6

Slide 10-7

Slide 10-8

Slide 10-9

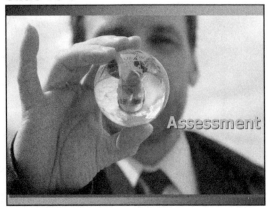

Slide 10-10

Slide 10-11

Slide 10-12

Slide 10-13

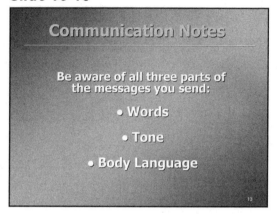

Slide 10-14

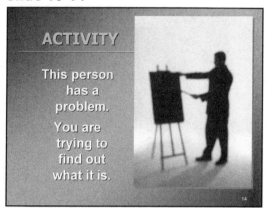

Slide 10-15

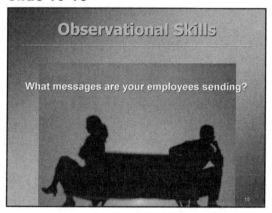

Slide 10-16

Slide 10-17

Slide 10-18

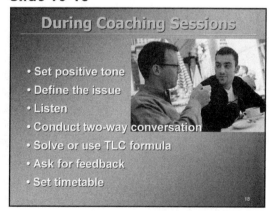

Slide 10-19

Slide 10-20

Slide 10-21

Slide 10-22

Slide 10-23

Slide 10-24

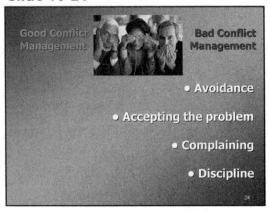

Slide 10-25

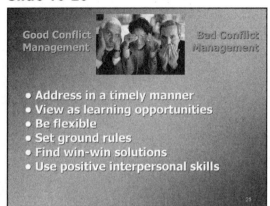

Slide 10-26

Slide 10-27

Slide 10-28

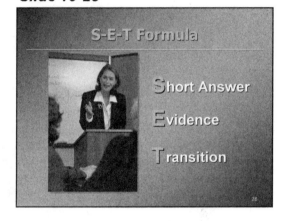

Slide 10-29

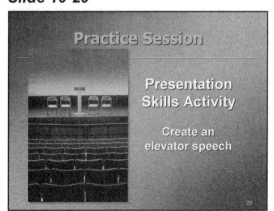

Slide 10-30

Slide 10-31

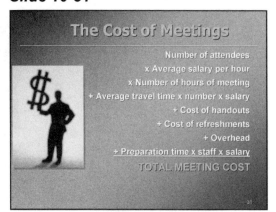

Slide 10-32

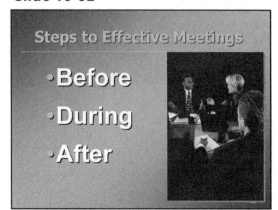

Slide 10-33

Slide 10-34

Slide 10-35

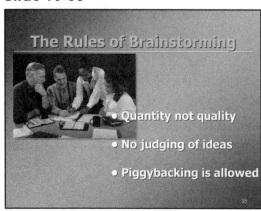

Slide 10-36

Slide 10-37

Side 10-38

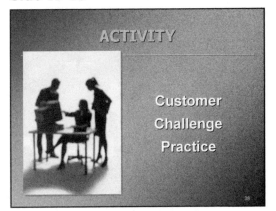

Slide 10-39

Slide 10-40

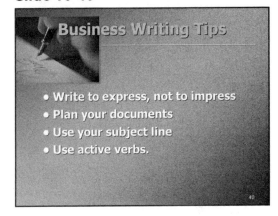

Slide 10-41

Slide 10-41

Slide 10-43

Slide 10-44

Slide 10-45

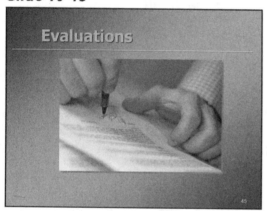

Slide 10-46

Slide 10-47

Slide 10-48

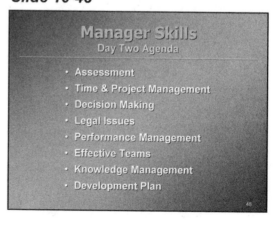

Slide 10-49

Slide 10-50

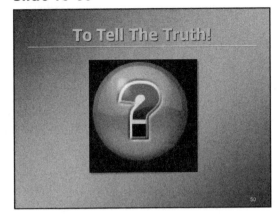

Slide 10-51

Slide 10-52

Slide 10-53

Slide 10-54

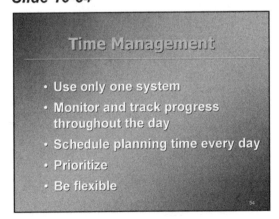

Slide 10-55

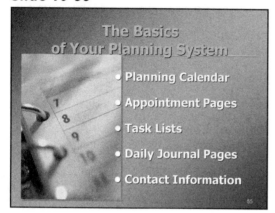

Slide 10-56

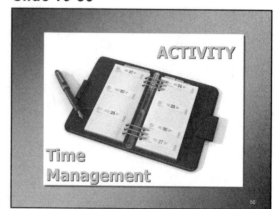

Slide 10-57

Slide 10-58

Slide 10-59

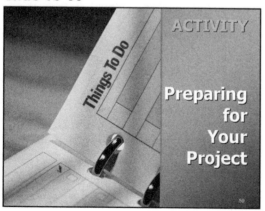

Slide 10-60

Slide 10-61

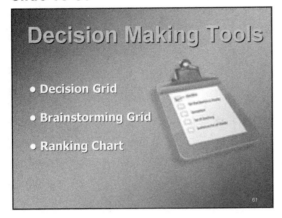

Slide 10-62

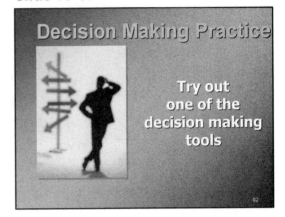

Slide 10-63

Slide 10-64

Slide 10-65

Slide 10-66

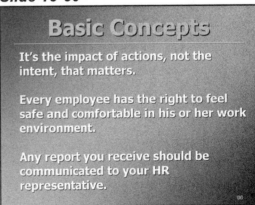

Slide 10-67

Slide 10-68

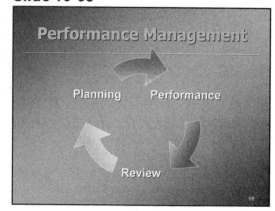

Slide 10-69

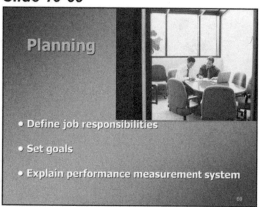

Slide 10-70

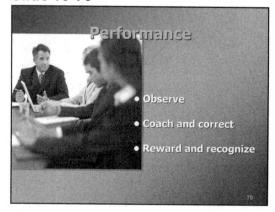

Slide 10-71

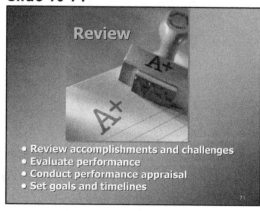

Slide 10-72

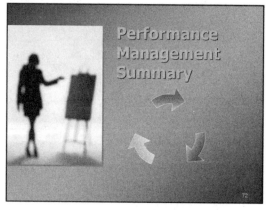

Slide 10-73

Performance
Appraisals

Slide 10-74

Performance
Appraisals

- Do your homework
- Schedule the session
- Make employee comfortable
- Start meeting positively
- Let employee talk
- Discuss appraisal ratings
- Discuss challenges
- Set goals and standards

Slide 10-75

Performance
Appraisal
Practice

Slide 10-76

Creating Teams

Slide 10-77

The Components
of Effective Teams

- Challenges
- Ground Rules
- Opportunities for
Performance & Learning
- Diversity

Slide 10-78

ACTIVITY

Teamwork Practice

Slide 10-79

Slide 10-80

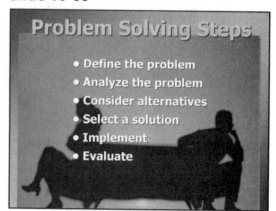

Slide 10-81

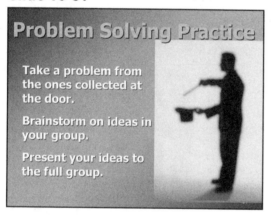

Slide 10-82

Slide 10-83

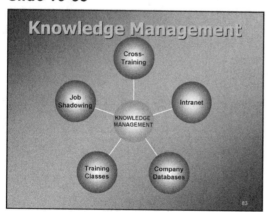

Slide 10-84

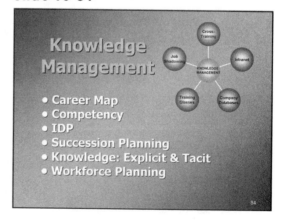

Slide 10-85

Slide 10-86

Slide 10-87

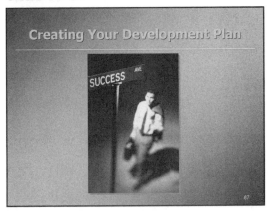

Slide 10-88

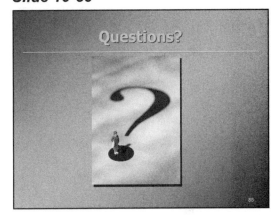

Slide 10-89

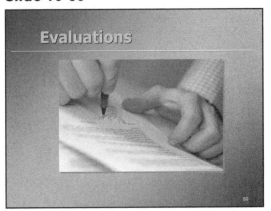

Slide 10-90

Learning Activities

- Tips for trainers

- Objectives, materials lists, and timeframes for the 20 learning activities used for these workshop formats

- Detailed instructions for conducting each learning activity

This chapter contains the following learning activities used in the various Manager Skills workshop formats:

- Learning Activity 11–1: Introductions

- Learning Activity 11–2: The Best Manager I Ever Knew . . .

- Learning Activity 11–3: Interpersonal Skills Practice

- Learning Activity 11–4: Coaching Session Dos and Don'ts

- Learning Activity 11–5: Motivating Employees

- Learning Activity 11–6: Resolving Conflict

- Learning Activity 11–7: Presentation Skills

- Learning Activity 11–8: Effective Meeting Exercise

- Learning Activity 11–9: Customer Service Practice

- Learning Activity 11–10: Business Writing Practice

- Learning Activity 11–11: Q&A Review Session

- Learning Activity 11–12: To Tell the Truth! Review

- Learning Activity 11–13: Time Management Exercise

- Learning Activity 11–14: Project Management Exercise

- Learning Activity 11–15: Decision Charts

- Learning Activity 11–16: Legal Issues

- Learning Activity 11–17: Performance Appraisal Practice

- Learning Activity 11–18: Creating Teams

- Learning Activity 11–19: Problem Solving Activity

- Learning Activity 11–20: Development Plan

Use this chapter in combination with the agenda chapter for your specific workshop format as a facilitator's guide when presenting each session.

Using the Website

You will find the learning activities, tools, training instruments, slides, and other materials included in this chapter on the website that accompanies this workbook. To access these files, go to www.ASTD.org/ManagerSkillsTraining and click on the following file names:

- *Assessment* [number].*pdf*

- *Tool* [number].*pdf*

- *Training Instrument* [number].*pdf*

- *One-Hour.ppt*

- *Half-Day.ppt*

- *One-Day.ppt*

- *Two-Day.ppt.*

To print out the materials for your training session, follow these simple steps. Click on the appropriate .pdf file name to open it in Adobe Acrobat software. Print out the pages of the document(s) needed for your training session.

For additional instructions on using the website, see the Appendix, "Using the Website," at the end of the workbook.

Tips for Trainers

Before using these learning activities in your training sessions, be sure to review chapters 1 through 4 for background on how this training program was developed. Chapter 5 included tips on facilitation, including preparation, room setup, and how to address the flow of the session.

As in all training, adding your personal touch by sharing your own stories will help make the content come alive. Feel free to describe your experiences with good and bad service whenever those examples might be helpful. Customizing the learning activities with examples from your organization (or the trainees' organization, if you are a consultant) also will add value to the program.

Be flexible. The timeframes for many of these activities can be changed according to your own goals and needs. You may find that you cover key concepts in the course of discussion and that you no longer need to include certain activities or content modules.

Learning Activity 11–1: Introductions

OBJECTIVE

The objective of this learning activity is to

◆ allow learners to become familiar with each other and with the manager skills that will be discussed in the workshop.

MATERIALS

For this activity, you will need

◆ flipchart and markers.

TIME

◆ 15 minutes

INSTRUCTIONS

1. Instruct learners to find someone in the room whom they don't know well so they can meet this person and introduce him or her to the rest of the group.

2. Tell them they will have three minutes to interview their partner. They should find out basics such as name and position, but they should also discover a managerial skill that this person does well. Give them some ideas of skills such as speaking, listening, delegating, coaching, leading, project management, and other managerial skills.

3. After three minutes, call time and have them switch roles.

4. After three more minutes, call time and ask for volunteers to introduce their partners.

5. As they are introduced, list the managerial skills that are discussed on the flipchart.

6. Continue until everyone has been introduced.

7. Conduct a debriefing discussion, using the following questions.

DISCUSSION QUESTIONS FOR DEBRIEFING

- ◆ Do you see other skills on this list that you have?

- ◆ Do you see some skills that you'd like to work on?

Learning Activity 11–2: The Best Manager I Ever Knew. . .

OBJECTIVE

The objective of this learning activity is to

◆ determine the traits of effective managers.

DOWNLOADS

MATERIALS

For this activity, you will need

◆ Training Instrument 12–1: The Best Manager I Ever Knew . . .

◆ flipchart pages and markers

◆ masking tape for each group to post pages.

TIME

◆ 20 minutes

INSTRUCTIONS

1. Divide the class into four groups. Give each group a flipchart page and marker.

2. Instruct them to appoint a scribe to keep notes for their group. The scribe will create a chart with two columns on their flipchart page. One column will be titled "Skills." The second column will be titled "Behaviors."

3. Ask each group to think about good managers they have known. As they describe these managers, the scribe will list the skills that made these managers outstanding in the first column. Then they will list one specific behavior that demonstrated this skill in the second column. For example, column one may note that the manager had excellent communication skills. Column two could note that the

manager stopped all other activities and actively listened when talking to an employee.

4. At the end of 10 minutes, each group will tape their page to the wall and present the information. Instruct others to list the skills discussed on Training Instrument 12–1. In column one they are to underline any of those traits they'd like to develop.

5. After each presentation, conduct a debriefing discussion, using the following questions.

DISCUSSION QUESTIONS FOR DEBRIEFING

◆ Are some of these skills ones that you think you do well?

◆ Did any of these spark ideas about other skills you'd like to develop?

Learning Activity 11–3: Interpersonal Skills Practice

OBJECTIVE

The objective of this learning activity is to

- ◆ practice using active listening and interpersonal skills to get to the root of a problem.

MATERIALS

DOWNLOADS

For this activity, you will need

- ◆ Training Instrument 12–2: Interpersonal Skills, one copy for each learner.

TIME

- ◆ 40 minutes

INSTRUCTIONS

1. Divide the class into groups of three.

2. Distribute copies of Training Instrument 12–2.

3. In each group, one person will be the person with a problem, one person will be the interviewer trying to understand what the problem is, and one person will be the observer.

4. Ask which group members will be the people with a problem. Explain that their problem is that they don't want to be here today. They can decide their own reason for that, such as they already know it all, they have too much to do, they once had a bad experience in a workshop, or they're depressed over something that happened this morning. Tell them that they will express their dislike for being here, but they are going to be reluctant to tell why. They should make their questioner work to find out that reason.

5. Ask for the people who will be trying to understand the problem. Tell them they are the interviewers. Their goal is to seek out information and to get the other person to discuss his or her problem by using active listening techniques.

6. Ask who are the observers. Their role is to use the training instrument and take notes about what they observe that each person does during the exercise.

7. Explain that they will have five minutes to conduct this conversation and at the end of that time, the observer will discuss his or her notes.

8. Conduct the exercise. At the end of five minutes, call time and allow the observers to lead their group debriefings for five minutes by discussing the notes they took.

9. Repeat two more rounds so that every attendee has an opportunity to perform each role.

10. After the exercise, conduct a debriefing discussion, using the following questions.

DISCUSSION QUESTIONS FOR DEBRIEFING

◆ What were some of the most effective listening techniques you saw demonstrated?

◆ During our workday, what are the things that keep us from doing a good job in these listening situations?

◆ Which skills did you observe that you can use to practice more effective listening skills with your employees?

Learning Activity 11–4: Coaching Session Dos and Don'ts

OBJECTIVE

The objective of this learning activity is to

DOWNLOADS

◆ create a list of dos and don'ts for coaching sessions.

MATERIALS

For this activity, you will need

◆ Training Instrument 12–3: Coaching Skills, one copy for each learner

◆ Tool 12–1: Coaching Notes, one copy for each learner.

TIME

◆ 20 minutes

INSTRUCTIONS

1. Divide the class into four groups.

2. Assign each group one of the scenarios on Training Instrument 12–4.

3. Give them 10 minutes to come up with a list of dos and don'ts for this particular session. They can get ideas from their personal experiences and by using Tool 12–1. Have them create their list on a flipchart page.

4. Each group will present its list and discussion points while the rest of the class takes notes, using the space on Training Instrument 12–4.

5. After the exercise, conduct a debriefing discussion, using the following questions.

DISCUSSION QUESTIONS FOR DEBRIEFING

- ◆ Do you have any recommendations to add to these lists?

- ◆ What do you think are the biggest downfalls of coaching in the workplace?

- ◆ What is something you will use from these lists?

Learning Activity 11–5: Motivating Employees

OBJECTIVE

The objective of this learning activity is to

◆ rank the motivators for employees and create ideas that incorporate these motivators.

MATERIALS

For this activity, you will need

DOWNLOADS

◆ Training Instrument 12–4: Motivating Employees, one copy for each learner

◆ flipchart pages and markers

◆ masking tape for each group to post pages.

TIME

◆ 20 minutes

INSTRUCTIONS

1. Divide participants into three groups.

2. Distribute copies of Training Instrument 12–4: Motivating Employees.

3. Assign each group one of the top motivators. The groups have 10 minutes to brainstorm ways to use this motivator in the workplace and list their ideas on a flipchart page to present to the class. For example, if their motivator is praise, perhaps the group would recommend an employee-of–the-month program, employee certificates, a bulletin board for customer compliments, and other recognition ideas.

4. Each group will present its idea lists. Instruct others to list the ideas on their training instruments, so they will have ideas to build on when they get back into their departments.

5. After each presentation, conduct a debriefing discussion, using these questions.

DISCUSSION QUESTIONS FOR DEBRIEFING

◆ Did you hear some ideas that will work in your situation?

◆ Did any of these spark other ideas you could use?

◆ Which of these ideas would motivate you?

Learning Activity 11–6: Resolving Conflict

OBJECTIVE

The objective of this learning activity is to

- practice the skills of conflict resolution by addressing a specific situation and proposing solutions.

DOWNLOADS

MATERIALS

For this activity, you will need

- Training Instrument 12–5: Resolving Conflict, one copy for each learner

- Tool 12–2: Conflict Management Strategies, one copy for each learner

- flipchart pages and markers

- masking tape for each group to post pages.

TIME

- 25 minutes

INSTRUCTIONS

1. Divide the class into four groups.

2. Assign one of the scenarios on Training Instrument 12–5 to each group.

3. Give them 10 minutes to come up with a list of ideas to address this conflict. They'll get some ideas by using Tool 12–2. Have them create their list on a flipchart page.

4. Each group will present its list and discussion points while the rest of the class takes notes, using the space on Training Instrument 12–5.

5. After the exercise, conduct a debriefing discussion, using these questions.

DISCUSSION QUESTIONS FOR DEBRIEFING

◆ Do you have any recommendations to add to these lists?

◆ What do you think are the biggest challenges to resolving work-place conflicts?

◆ What is something you will use from these lists?

Learning Activity 11–7: Presentation Skills

OBJECTIVE

The objective of this learning activity is to

- practice condensing a message to its most important elements while conducting a review of the topics covered earlier in the workshop.

DOWNLOADS

MATERIALS

For this activity, you will need

- Training Instrument 12–6: Presentation Skills, one copy for each learner.

TIME

- 40 minutes

INSTRUCTIONS

1. Distribute copies of Training Instrument 12–6.

2. They will now practice the SET formula of presentation skills. That formula includes Short answer, Evidence, and a Transition statement. Each person will choose one topic and condense that answer into an elevator speech of no more than 60 seconds.

3. Participants will practice on partners in the room and make revisions based on input. At the end of the 15 minutes, each person will stand and present his or her elevator speech to the rest of the class.

4. After the presentations, conduct a debriefing discussion, using these questions.

DISCUSSION QUESTIONS FOR DEBRIEFING

- Why do you think we practiced doing a short talk instead of a long one?

◆ What ideas did you get from these presentations about ways to present your information effectively?

◆ What about this process is challenging to you?

◆ When do you think would be good times to use an elevator speech?

Learning Activity 11–8: Effective Meeting Exercise

OBJECTIVE

The objective of this learning activity is to

♦ produce a comprehensive meeting plan based on specific criteria.

MATERIALS

DOWNLOADS

For this activity, you will need

♦ Training Instrument 12–7: Effective Meetings, one copy for each learner

♦ Tool 12–4: Agenda Form, one copy for each learner

♦ Tool 12–5: Meeting Planning Form, one copy for each learner

♦ Tool 12–6: Minutes Format, one copy for each learner

♦ flipchart pages and markers

♦ masking tape for each group to post pages.

TIME

♦ 20 minutes

INSTRUCTIONS

1. Divide the class into three groups.

2. Distribute copies of Training Instrument 12–7 and Tools 12–4, 12–5, 12–6.

3. Explain that each group will create part of a meeting plan on the supplied flipchart page. The purpose and background information about the meeting is on the training instrument. You will assign one task to each group. One group will use page one of the Agenda Form to create the agenda for the meeting. Another group will use page two of the Agenda Form to create the email to announce the meeting.

The other group will use the Meeting Planning Form to decide the room setup and what materials should be created for the meeting. They will have 10 minutes to decide what to do for the items listed on the form.

4. Each group will present its part of the meeting plan to the rest of the class. Every person in the group is required to participate in the presentation.

5. After each presentation, conduct a debriefing discussion with the team and the rest of the class, using these questions.

DISCUSSION QUESTIONS FOR DEBRIEFING

◆ What other considerations do you think might need to be addressed about this particular part of planning a meeting?

Learning Activity 11–9: Customer Service Practice

OBJECTIVE

The objective of this learning activity is to

◆ practice the steps of resolving customer challenges.

DOWNLOADS

MATERIALS

For this activity, you will need

◆ Training Instrument 12–8: Customer Service, one copy for each learner

◆ Tool 12–8: Customer Service Formula, one copy for each learner.

TIME

◆ 25 minutes

INSTRUCTIONS

1. Divide the class into three groups.

2. Distribute copies of Training Instrument 12–8 and Tool 12–8.

3. Assign one of the customer service scenarios to each group.

4. Each group will create a five-minute presentation showing how they would handle this scenario. Allow them five minutes for this process.

5. The groups will then present their best ideas for how to handle this situation by simulating the situation. (If you have additional time and a group that is very interactive, you can offer them the option of showing the wrong way and then the right way to handle the situation. This can help loosen up a group that's less interactive. Besides, it's just funny . . .)

6. Conduct the exercise. Remind the participants to take notes of phrases they like, methods they think are effective, and any other notes on the Training Instrument.

7. After each presentation, conduct a debriefing discussion, using the questions provided.

DISCUSSION QUESTIONS FOR DEBRIEFING

◆ What methods did you see that you liked in this presentation?

◆ Do you have any other ideas that might work in a situation like this?

Learning Activity 11–10: Business Writing Practice

OBJECTIVE

The objective of this learning activity is to

◆ demonstrate the skills of creating effective written communication.

DOWNLOADS

MATERIALS

For this activity, you will need

◆ Training Instrument 12–9: Business Writing, one copy for each learner

TIME

◆ 40 minutes

INSTRUCTIONS

1. Divide participants into four groups.

2. Distribute copies of Training Instrument 12–9. Assign one of the situations to each group.

3. Using the information you have discussed on effective written communications, each person will follow the instructions on the training instrument and construct an email to address the given situation. Allow 10 minutes for this process.

4. Once they have completed the email, each participant will read it to the others in their group for critique. Allow 10 minutes for this step.

5. Each group will choose one to be presented to the full class.

6. After each presentation, conduct a debriefing discussion with the class, using the questions provided.

DISCUSSION QUESTIONS FOR DEBRIEFING

◆ What did you like about this email?

◆ What would you like to see done differently in this email?

Learning Activity 11–11: Q&A Review Session

OBJECTIVE

The objective of this learning activity is to

- allow learners to review the materials that have been discussed in the workshop.

MATERIALS

For this activity, you will need

- timer

- one index card per person

- flipchart and markers.

TIME

- 20 minutes

INSTRUCTIONS

1. Divide the class into two teams. You can allow the teams to create their own names or you can simply give them names such as the Blue Team and the Red Team.

2. Instruct each person to write one question on the card based on the materials that have been discussed during the day. These will be questions for the other team to try to answer. These should not be true/false or trick questions. They may use their notes. They may discuss these questions as a team. They have five minutes to compose all their questions. They will write the correct answer on the bottom of the cards. (This is important in case you forget a fact from the session. It happens!)

3. Draw two columns on a flipchart page and label one column for each team.

4. Collect the cards from each group. You will call out the questions from one group to the other group. The group will try to answer the questions as a team. Add a check to the team's column for each question they get correct. Move quickly through the questions. This is a timed event.

5. After five minutes, call time and call out questions to the other team. If some of the questions are the same as those asked of the other team, you may omit them.

6. When time is through, add up the checks to determine the winning team.

7. If you have more time, you can call out the remaining questions for an additional review. (As an alternate format, you can rotate back and forth between teams with one question at a time.)

8. Conduct a debriefing discussion, using these questions.

DISCUSSION QUESTIONS FOR DEBRIEFING

◆ Do you have questions about any of the information from this game?

◆ Did these bring to mind any other questions that you'd like answered?

Learning Activity 11–12: To Tell the Truth! Review

OBJECTIVE

The objective of this learning activity is to

 ◆ reinforce materials that were discussed in the previous workshop.

MATERIALS

 ◆ none

TIME

 ◆ 15 minutes

INSTRUCTIONS

1. Ask each person to think of three facts that were discussed in the previous session. Two will be correct, one should be false. They are going to try to fool the room in the style of the old game show "To Tell the Truth." (Don't admit if you're old enough to remember the television show!)

2. Each person will stand and say his or her three statements. The group will guess which one is incorrect. They will correct the statement if they know the right information.

3. Conduct a debriefing discussion, using these questions.

DISCUSSION QUESTIONS FOR DEBRIEFING

 ◆ Do you have questions about any of these statements?

 ◆ Did you remember more than you thought you would?

Learning Activity 11–13: Time Management Exercise

OBJECTIVE

The objective of this learning activity is to

- ◆ apply the rules of time management to determine the priority of standard daily tasks.

DOWNLOADS

MATERIALS

For this activity, you will need

- ◆ Training Instrument 12–10: Time Management, one copy for each learner

- ◆ Tool 12–10: Time Management, one copy for each learner.

TIME

- ◆ 20 minutes

INSTRUCTIONS

1. Divide class into four groups.

2. Distribute copies of Training Instrument 12–10.

3. Hand out one copy of Tool 12–10 to each group.

4. Each group will follow the instructions on the Training Instrument to practice prioritizing duties based on time-management principles. Their goal will be to prioritize the list of tasks based on their urgency and value to the organization.

5. After the activity, conduct a debriefing discussion with the team and the rest of the class, using the questions provided.

DISCUSSION QUESTIONS FOR DEBRIEFING

- ◆ Was there any disagreement in your group about the order of your prioritized items?

◆ What helped you determine the order of priority?

◆ How can you teach your staff to prioritize projects and tasks?

Learning Activity 11–14: Project Management Exercise

OBJECTIVE

The objective of this learning activity is to

◆ generate a project management plan using a structured, step-by-step process.

DOWNLOADS

MATERIALS

For this activity, you will need

◆ Training Instrument 12–11: Project Management Chart, one copy for each learner

◆ Tool 12–11: Project Management, one copy for each learner

◆ flipchart pages and markers

◆ masking tape for each group to post pages.

TIME

◆ 30 minutes

INSTRUCTIONS

1. Divide group into three teams.

2. Distribute copies of Training Instrument 12–11 and Tool 12–11.

3. Assign one scenario to each group.

4. Explain that they will now take this project from start to finish, using the flipchart pages to document each stage. For example, they will brainstorm on the steps of the project on one flipchart page. Then they will number those steps. On the next page, they will create a chart of responsibilities and deadlines. They will then add follow-up activities to their chart to evaluate the project. At the end of the 15 minutes, each group will have five minutes to present its plan to the

rest of the class. Everyone in the group is required to participate in the presentation.

5. After all the groups have presented, conduct a debriefing discussion with the class, using these questions.

DISCUSSION QUESTIONS FOR DEBRIEFING

◆   What were the most difficult parts of this exercise?

◆   What worked well in your group?

◆   How did the different deadlines affect your project management?

◆   What if you wanted to create a project plan in a virtual meeting? Any ideas how this process might be done online?

Learning Activity 11–15: Decision Charts

OBJECTIVE

The objective of this learning activity is to

- demonstrate the steps of three different methods of decision making.

MATERIALS

DOWNLOADS

For this activity, you will need

- Training Instrument 12–12: Decision Charts, one copy for each learner

- Tool 12–12: Decision Grid, one copy for each learner

- Tool 12–13: Decision Chart, one copy for each learner

- Tool 12–14: Assessment Chart, one copy for each learner

- flipchart pages and markers

- masking tape for each group to post pages.

TIME

- 20 minutes

INSTRUCTIONS

1. Distribute copies of Training Instrument 12–12 and Tools 12–12, 12–13, 12–14.

2. Assign one of the methods to each group. Their task is to demonstrate how to use the method to the rest of the participants.

3. Give them 10 minutes to prepare.

4. Allow five minutes per team for presentations.

5. Conduct a debriefing discussion, using the questions provided.

DISCUSSION QUESTIONS FOR DEBRIEFING

◆ What are some ways you could use each of these methods?

◆ How could you adapt these for individual decision making?

Learning Activity 11–16: Legal Issues

OBJECTIVE

The objective of this learning activity is to

DOWNLOADS

- ◆ gain understanding of the various legal issues that participants can face in their roles as managers.

MATERIALS

For this activity, you will need

- ◆ Training Instrument 12–13: Test Your Knowledge, one copy for each learner.

TIME

- ◆ 25 minutes

INSTRUCTIONS

1. Distribute copies of Training Instrument 12–13.

2. Give participants 10 minutes to answer the questions.

3. Conduct a debriefing discussion, using these answers to the questions.

4. Be sure to review this information frequently with your legal counsel or human resources department as laws change frequently and new precedents are being set every day.

DISCUSSION QUESTION ANSWERS FOR DEBRIEFING

1. The company is liable in cases of employment law violations, not the manager. False. Not only the company, but the manager can be found liable in employee lawsuits.

2. *Quid pro quo* is a form of sexual harassment. True. *Quid pro quo* (Translation: This for that) means getting consideration in return for sexual favors.

3. Asking only male employees to move heavy boxes could be considered discrimination. True. Certainly male employees often offer to lift heavy items, but it cannot be restricted to them unless it is a specific part of their job description. Remember, anything that singles out different genders, races, backgrounds, and so forth, from others is discriminating behavior.

4. Harassment from customers can be grounds for a harassment claim by an employee. True. Absolutely. An employee should feel safe and comfortable in his or her workplace. Whether harassment comes from another employee, a customer, or even a vendor, it is grounds for a harassment suit.

5. Supervisors should inform upper management about sexual harassment allegations only if they were not able to handle the allegations themselves. False. You're taking on extra liability if you don't forward allegations to human resources or your manager. This information should never stop with you.

6. In a job interview, you can ask a person if he or she has been arrested. False. You can ask if a person has been convicted, but not arrested.

7. In a job interview, you can ask a person if he or she has children. False. It is not relevant. All that is relevant is that the person can commit to the hours and responsibilities of the position.

8. The following question is legal in a job interview: "To what clubs or social organizations do you belong?" False. There may be a bias based on a social organization. You can ask them what professional organizations they belong to because those are directly related to their jobs.

9. The following question is legal in a job interview: "What language did you speak in your home when you were growing up?" False. This forces a person to reveal his or her nationality or ethnic background and cannot be considered in a job interview.

10. It is the impact, not the intent of actions that matters in harassment cases. True. This is one of the most important things to keep in mind. It doesn't work to say "I was just joking" or "That's not how I meant it." Your intent doesn't matter. It's how the other person receives the message or action. When in doubt, don't say or do it!

Learning Activity 11–17: Performance Appraisal Practice

OBJECTIVE

The objective of this learning activity is to

- practice the steps of an effective performance appraisal.

DOWNLOADS

MATERIALS

For this activity, you will need

- Training Instrument 12–14: Performance Appraisals, one copy for each learner

- Tool 12–16: Performance Management Process, one copy for each learner.

TIME

- 45 minutes

INSTRUCTIONS

1. Divide the class into groups of three.

2. Distribute copies of Training Instrument 12–14.

3. Ask the groups to review the performance appraisal situation listed on their training instruments. In each group, each person will get an opportunity to be the manager, the employee, and the observer.

4. Give them 15 minutes to prepare for the roles.

5. Each group will practice the performance appraisal. The manager will discuss, the employee will react as he or she sees fit, and the observer will take notes, using Tool 12–16.

6. After nine minutes, call time. Ask the observer to discuss his or her notes with the group. Those who were practicing the appraisal will

also be able to make comments. Allow nine minutes for this discussion, then instruct participants to change roles.

7. After nine more minutes, call time, repeat the discussion process.

8. Have them take the remaining roles they have not yet played and repeat the process.

9. After the exercise, conduct a debriefing discussion, using these questions.

DISCUSSION QUESTIONS FOR DEBRIEFING

◆ Did you see some practices that seemed to work well for these appraisals?

◆ What were some of the best phrases you heard our managers use?

◆ What is something you learned from this practice?

Learning Activity 11–18: Creating Teams

OBJECTIVE

The objective of this learning activity is to

◆ create a plan to maximize the effectiveness of the personalities and skills of the team members.

DOWNLOADS

MATERIALS

For this activity, you will need

◆ Training Instrument 12–15: Creating Teams, one copy for each learner

◆ flipchart pages and markers

◆ masking tape for each group to post pages.

TIME

◆ 35 minutes

INSTRUCTIONS

1. Distribute copies of Training Instrument 12–15.

2. Assign one Team Personality to each group.

3. Explain that they have 15 minutes to consider the information they have on their team member's personality type and determine how to work effectively with that personality to help teams achieve their goals.

4. They will deliver a presentation on why that personality is valuable to a team and the dos and don'ts of working with that personality type.

5. After each presentation, conduct a debriefing discussion with the team and the rest of the class, using the questions provided.

DISCUSSION QUESTIONS FOR DEBRIEFING

◆ Do you have someone with this personality type on your team?

◆ Do you think you could use some of these ideas to work more effectively with this person?

◆ Do you have any methods that you've used to work effectively with someone of this personality type?

Learning Activity 11–19: Problem Solving Activity

OBJECTIVE

The objective of this learning activity is to

♦ practice the steps of solving a workplace challenge.

DOWNLOADS

MATERIALS

For this activity, you will need

♦ Training Instrument 12–16: Problem Solving, one copy for each learner

♦ Tool 12–18: Problem Solving, one copy for each learner

♦ box of problems "left at the door" at the beginning of the day.

TIME

♦ 30 minutes

INSTRUCTIONS

1. Divide the group into four "think tank" groups.

2. Distribute copies of Training Instrument 12–16 and Tool 12–18.

3. Introduce the exercise by noting that this is an opportunity to practice all of the things that have been discussed during the course of this workshop and to solve a real problem for one of their fellow attendees.

4. Ask each person to pull a problem out of the box of challenges.

5. Give participants 15 minutes to study the challenge, discuss ideas with others in their group, and brainstorm possible solutions.

6. Each person will have an opportunity to read his or her situation and share his or her best idea for handling this situation in the form of an elevator speech.

7. After each item is discussed, ask others if they have had similar challenges and how they have handled them. This exercise can be adjusted in length by either allowing additional discussion or by eliminating this step.

8. After the exercise, conduct a debriefing discussion, using these questions.

DISCUSSION QUESTIONS FOR DEBRIEFING

◆ Did you hear some ideas that might work for the challenges that you have?

◆ What are some ways you could adapt some of these solutions to address other challenges?

Learning Activity 11–20: Development Plan

OBJECTIVE

The objective of this learning activity is to

DOWNLOADS

- ◆ begin creation of an individual development plan to continue expansion of managerial skills.

MATERIALS

For this activity, you will need

- ◆ Training Instrument 12–17: Development Plan, one copy for each learner

- ◆ Tool 12–20: Individual Development Plan, one copy for each learner.

TIME

- ◆ 10 minutes

INSTRUCTIONS

1. Distribute copies of Training Instrument 12–17 and Tool 12–20.

2. Introduce this exercise by assuring them that you don't expect them to create a complete development plan in just 10 minutes. This is an opportunity for them to begin creating a plan that they will continue building when they have their own private strategic-planning sessions.

3. Refer to the instructions on the training instrument.

4. Ask each individual to consider the material that has been discussed and the results of the assessments he or she completed earlier in the workshop.

5. They should choose one area they'd like to focus on first and list one thing they can do in the next week to begin working on their development in that area.

6. After the exercise, conduct a debriefing discussion, using these questions.

DISCUSSION QUESTIONS FOR DEBRIEFING

◆ Would someone like to share what he or she will be working on?

◆ What actions are you going to take in the next week to get started?

◆

Training Instruments, Assessments, and Tools

What's in This Chapter

- ◆ Handouts and forms to be used in conjunction with the 20 learning activities used in these workshop formats

This chapter contains the following materials used in the various Manager Skills workshop formats (see Appendix):

- ◆ Training Instrument 12–1: The Best Manager I Ever Knew . . .
- ◆ Training Instrument 12–2: Interpersonal Skills
- ◆ Training Instrument 12–3: Coaching Skills
- ◆ Training Instrument 12–4: Motivating Employees
- ◆ Training Instrument 12–5: Resolving Conflict
- ◆ Training Instrument 12–6: Presentation Skills
- ◆ Training Instrument 12–7: Effective Meetings
- ◆ Training Instrument 12–8: Customer Service
- ◆ Training Instrument 12–9: Business Writing
- ◆ Training Instrument 12–10: Time Management
- ◆ Training Instrument 12–11: Project Management Chart
- ◆ Training Instrument 12–12: Decision Charts
- ◆ Training Instrument 12–13: Legal Issues
- ◆ Training Instrument 12–14: Performance Appraisals

- Training Instrument 12–15: Creating Teams

- Training Instrument 12–16: Problem Solving

- Training Instrument 12–17: Development Plan

- Assessment 12–1: Manager Self-Assessment

- Assessment 12–2: Evaluation Form

- Tool 12–1: Coaching Notes

- Tool 12–2: Conflict Management Strategies

- Tool 12–3: Presentation Design Form

- Tool 12–4: Agenda Form

- Tool 12–5: Meeting Planning Form

- Tool 12–6: Minutes Format

- Tool 12–7: Brainstorming

- Tool 12–8: Customer Service Formula

- Tool 12–9: Business Writing Tips

- Tool 12–10: Time Management

- Tool 12–11: Project Management

- Tool 12–12: Decision Grid

- Tool 12–13: Decision Chart

- Tool 12–14: Assessment Chart

- Tool 12–15: Recordkeeping

- Tool 12–16: Performance Management Process

- Tool 12–17: Performance Appraisals

- Tool 12–18: Problem Solving

- Tool 12–19: Knowledge Management

- Tool 12–20: Individual Development Plan

Training Instrument 12-1

The Best Manager I Ever Knew . . .

SKILLS OF OUTSTANDING MANAGERS	BEHAVIORS THAT DEMONSTRATED THESE SKILLS

Training Instrument 12–2

Interpersonal Skills

As you observe the exchange, check the items below that the interviewer performs well. Make note of specific phrases, nonverbal methods, and other communication techniques that are effective. Also, note any cues that the other person sends out that the interviewer might have missed.

OBSERVER FORM

INTERVIEWER:	OBSERVER:
Which techniques did the interviewer use?	*What were the most effective questions the interviewer asked?*
Body language:	
❑ Maintained good eye contact	
❑ Gave nonverbal reinforcement	
❑ Maintained a relaxed posture	
❑ Used appropriate gestures	*What else worked well in this discussion?*
❑ Leaned toward the other person	
❑ Used effective facial expressions	
❑ Responded to nonverbal cues	
❑ *Specific notes:*	
	What did you observe that the interviewer might not have noticed? Did you think of anything else he/she might have tried in this situation?
Tone:	
❑ Used an effective tone of voice	
❑ Spoke at appropriate volume	**Body language:**
❑ Projected genuine concern	
❑ Used a nonintimidating tone	
❑ Spoke in a way that calmed the speaker	
❑ *Specific notes:*	**Tone:**
Words:	
❑ Gave verbal reinforcement	**Words:**
❑ Repeated to ensure understanding	
❑ Asked open-ended questions	
❑ Solicited examples	
❑ Used positive language	
❑ *Specific notes:*	

Training Instrument 12–3

Coaching Skills

COACHING SESSION DOS AND DON'TS

SCENARIOS	DOS AND DON'TS
A You are coaching someone who was an excellent employee, but over the past few months has become increasingly withdrawn and angry.	
B You are coaching an enthusiastic new employee who wants to rise in the organization, but has little patience and expects to be promoted immediately.	
C You are correcting an employee who has been with the organization longer than you have and is showing signs of frustration.	
D You are coaching an employee who has started procrastinating and becoming argumentative whenever you ask him/her to work on a specific project.	

Training Instrument 12–4

Motivating Employees

REWARD AND RECOGNITION BRAINSTORMING

TOP MOTIVATORS	REWARD AND RECOGNITION IDEAS USING THESE MOTIVATORS

Training Instrument 12–5

Resolving Conflict

CONFLICT PRACTICE SITUATIONS

Class practice situation: Mary comes back from vacation to discover that her silver frame is missing from her desk. She becomes argumentative and is going from desk to desk, searching through her coworkers' drawers, causing angry outbursts from more than one staff member.

1. Jeff has a habit of staying out at lunch a little too long. You hadn't really noticed because you are out at lunch at the same time, but Don has noticed because he can't leave for his lunch break until Jeff gets back. You walk back into the office to a situation that is close to a fist fight.

2. Cathy and David just can't get along. They work in adjoining cubicles and are constantly sniping at each other. You have addressed it, but it doesn't seem to have gotten any better. Now, others in the office are starting to feel they have to take sides and it's creating a hostile atmosphere.

3. Doris might as well open a store in her office. Every time her daughter's third-grade class has something to sell, she's got boxes of items and tries to sell to anyone who gets even close to her door. Now people are avoiding her office. That's really tricky, since it's next to your office.

4. You were promoted to manager of a department you've worked in for years. You have a lot of friends in the department and now you are finding that you can't associate with them in the same way you have in the past. Most of them understand, but a few of them are angry, and you even hear murmurs of "too good for us" and "power changed her."

Training Instrument 12–6

Presentation Skills

USING THE SET FORMULA

Use this column to make notes and brainstorm on the steps of SET.	*Use this column for the final wording of your SET answer.*
What is the basic answer to the question?	**Short Answer**
What are three points that support the basic answer?	**Evidence**
Summarize how the evidence supported your answer and transition the conversation back to the other person.	**Transition**

Training Instrument 12–7

Effective Meetings

EFFECTIVE MEETING EXERCISE

Your company has 10 managers and 100 frontline workers. You are going to announce a new software system for your company that will affect the way frontline workers perform their duties.

Assignment	*Notes*
Room Setup Whom would you invite to the meeting? How would you set up the room? What printed materials would you provide? What visual aids, equipment, or other tools might you use? What other considerations or arrangements might you need for this meeting?	
Meeting Communications Write a sample email to announce the meeting and determine whom it would be sent to.	
Agenda Draw up an agenda for this meeting and determine who would need to speak and what items should be covered in the meeting.	

Training Instrument 12–8

Customer Service

CUSTOMER SERVICE CHALLENGE

Using the practices of effective customer service, determine the best way to handle your group's situation. Your group will present your best ideas for handling this scenario by using a format such as a skit, presentation, or panel discussion.

A	B
This customer is angry. He's been sent to three different offices to get his problem resolved, and now he's ended up with your newest employee, who doesn't know how to handle this type of issue. Do you jump in and push the employee aside to fix the situation? Do you wait until he or she asks for help? Do you wait until the customer leaves? Do you send someone else in to fix the situation? What are your main concerns in this situation?	This customer has asked to see the manager. He has an outdated coupon. You don't want to undermine your employee, who is a senior staff member, but it is a policy to accept all coupons, no matter what the expiration date. How do you handle this situation?
C	**D**
You observe an employee repeatedly explaining something to a customer, but the customer can't understand what he or she is saying. You can tell that the employee is getting angry with the customer by his or her tone and volume. How do you correct the employee and ensure that the customer's needs are met without publicly chastising the employee?	The customer insists that he wants a copy of a file that is not allowed to leave your office. Your employee has told him or her this and now the customer wants to talk to you. Unfortunately, the employee apparently told the customer in an extremely rude manner and the situation has escalated to a shouting match. What strategies will you use to handle this situation?

Training Instrument 12–9

Business Writing

BUSINESS WRITING PRACTICE

Using the business writing tips, write an email for your group's situation from the four samples below. Write an email to address that situation. You will practice with others in your group and vote on the best email.

A	B
You are sending an email to tell your staff members that they will be attending a session on business writing next week.	Compose an email to explain to a customer that he or she is not entitled to receive a rebate because the offer has expired.

C	D
Write an email to announce a new workplace contest for sales in which the winner will receive an extra week of vacation.	You will write an email to explain a new dress-code policy that will eliminate casual Fridays in your workplace.

Training Instrument 12–10

Time Management

PRIORITIZE	
A, B, or C	*Prioritize the following items as A, B, or C. If you decide you need additional facts to make your decision, you can create them and add them to the Notes line under the task.*
	Call Fred to set appointment for this afternoon's meeting. Notes:
	Make flight reservations for business trip next month. Notes:
	Meet with staff on XYZ project due this Friday. Notes:
	Send emails to invitees for meeting next week. Notes:
	Schedule to attend time management seminar. Notes:
	Reschedule overdue doctor appointment. Notes:
	Proofread report that will be sent out tomorrow morning. Notes:
	Visit with staff members. Notes:
	Answer emails. Notes:
	Read article on new business contacts. Notes:

Training Instrument 12–11

Project Management Chart

Instructions:

- ◆ Brainstorm to determine all the steps of your project.
- ◆ Place the steps in order in the chart below.
- ◆ Estimate how long each action item will take.
- ◆ If time is limited, use reverse engineering to determine deadlines by starting with the completion date and then dating each action item from last to first. Remember that other tasks may need to be rescheduled to allow time for completion of this project.
- ◆ Adjust completion date if needed to ensure that you are not creating unrealistic goals.
- ◆ Assign responsibility for the task.
- ◆ Determine any additional resources that can help with this task.
- ◆ Notes column is optional. Notes can be recorded on this chart or in project folder.
- ◆ Tracking symbols include: ✓ Complete ✗ Delete *IP* In Progress

PROJECT MANAGEMENT CHART

TRACKING *Symbols:* ✓ Complete ✗ Delete *IP* In Progress	ACTION *Always starts with a verb.*	DEADLINE *Must be completed by . . .*	RESPONSIBLE *Who will do this?*	RESOURCES *What is needed? What can help with this task?*	NOTES *What needs to happen first? Other notes.*

Training Instrument 12–12

Decision Charts

DECISION CHARTS	
Make notes in this column about the different decision-making tools and how to use them.	*What's good about this method?* *What are some ideas of ways you could use this tool?* *How could you adapt this tool for other uses?*
Decision Grid (or Brainstorming Grid)	
Decision Chart	
Assessment Chart	

Training Instrument 12–13

Legal Issues

TRUE	FALSE	STATEMENT
		1. The company is liable in cases of employment law violations, not the manager.
		2. *Quid pro quo* is a form of sexual harassment.
		3. Asking only male employees to move heavy boxes could be considered discrimination.
		4. Harassment from customers can be grounds for a harassment claim by an employee.
		5. Supervisors should inform upper management about sexual harassment allegations only if they were not able to handle the allegations themselves.
		6. In a job interview, you can ask a person if he or she has been arrested.
		7. In a job interview, you can ask a person if he or she has children.
		8. The following question is legal in a job interview: To what clubs or social organizations do you belong?
		9. The following question is legal in a job interview: What language did you speak in your home when you were growing up?
		10. It is the impact, not the intent of actions that matters in harassment cases.

Training Instrument 12–14

Performance Appraisals

PERFORMANCE APPRAISAL PRACTICE

Manager Notes:

This employee has been excellent in the past, but recently has started performing poorly.

He/she has been late for work at least once a week for the past two months.

He/she has missed deadlines on two projects in the last month.

He/she has started exhibiting unusual behaviors such as negative comments, withdrawn and silent, and sitting at the computer staring into space.

However, before this period, he/she had been named Employee of the Month twice during the past year for going above and beyond in helping others in the office.

He/she had designed a new organizational system for the office that increased productivity by 10 percent.

He/she had taken three different classes in leadership and supervisory skills.

Employee Notes:
Refer to the above notes for what your situation is.

Decide your own reasons for the change in your behavior.

React as you see fit to any comments made by your manager.

Observer Notes:

Use the reminders below to determine what the manager does well. Check off items as he/she does them.

Make additional notes on any phrases you like that he/she uses, any body language, or gestures that are effective.

Be prepared to discuss this after the interaction is completed.

1. Do your homework.
2. Schedule the session, giving the employee enough time to prepare.
3. Make the employee comfortable with a private location and seating without a desk between you.
4. Start the meeting with a positive comment.
5. Let the employee talk, brag, vent, and so forth.
6. Discuss appraisal ratings with the employee.
7. Compare documented results to established performance standards.
8. Decide together what you can do to solve any challenges.
9. Communicate the performance standards of the next review period.
10. Record the goals so that you both can refer back to them for periodic appraisal.

Training Instrument 12–15

Creating Teams

TEAM PERSONALITIES

DRIVER

This Describes Me: I'm pretty direct when I talk to you about issues. Some people might see that as blunt. I think of myself as a problem solver. I don't mind taking risks or making decisions. Give me a situation and let me run with it.

When You Deal With Me, Do These Things: Get to the point. Stay focused on the business at hand. Give me the pros and cons.

Please Don't Do These Things: Don't ramble or make a lot of small talk. Don't focus on problems. Come to me with potential solutions. Don't be vague. Give me specifics. Don't make statements that you can't back up.

As a Team Player: I'm in control and great in a crisis. I'm innovative in getting results. I stay focused on goals. I am specific and direct. I can provide direction and leadership. I will push the team toward decisions. I am willing to speak out. I welcome challenges without fear and am willing to accept the risk. I'm a big-picture person.

Notes:

INFLUENCING

This Describes Me: I enjoy talking and communicating with others. I'm enthusiastic and optimistic. I'm trusting. I can be very persuasive. I have been known to be impulsive.

When You Deal With Me, Do These Things: Let me talk about my ideas and then help me come up with a plan to turn my talk into action. Ensure that we have time for discussion and sociable activities. Give me the details in writing so I can look at them later. Work with me as a partner. Come up with good recognition and reward plans to help me stay motivated.

Please Don't Do These Things: Don't eliminate social time. Don't do all the talking. Don't ignore my ideas or downplay my accomplishments. Don't tell me what to do; instead work with me to create a plan of action.

As a Team Player: I'm a creative problem solver. I'm a motivator, communicator, and peacemaker. I'm good at working with the team to accomplish goals. I'm agreeable and respond well to the unexpected. I like to create a comfortable atmosphere for the team. I have a good sense of humor.

Notes:

continued on next page

Training Instrument 12–15, continued

Creating Teams

STEADY

This Describes Me: I'm a steady, stable worker. I'm a good listener and a great team player. I take ownership of my projects. I'm understanding and friendly to my co-workers. I'm pretty predictable in my actions.

When You Deal With Me, Do These Things: Create a favorable environment for discussion by being personal and agreeable. Express a genuine interest in me as a person. Explain tasks specifically. Talk to me to find out my goals. If we have to go through change, present the information to me in a nonthreatening manner and give me a little time to adjust to the idea. Explain our team goals to me clearly and my role in achieving those goals. Assure me that I'll have your support.

Don't Do These Things: Don't be pushy with your ideas or demands. Don't be overly aggressive or demanding. Don't be too confrontational.

As a Team Player: You can count on me—I'm reliable and dependable. I'm a loyal team player and I follow the rules. I'm a good listener, I am patient, and I can help you resolve conflicts. With good common sense, I can often see an easier way of doing things. I'm focused and have a good sense of people and relationships. I'm pretty even tempered and provide stability on the team. I'm patient, realistic, and practical.

Notes:

COMPLIANT

This Describes Me: I pride myself on being accurate and detail-oriented. I'm analytical and like to work with organized systems. I'm conscientious and careful. I'm a fact finder. I'm organized and precise in my work. I have high standards of quality.

When You Deal With Me, Do These Things: Prepare your case in advance with accurate data. Submit an exact job description with a precise explanation of how that task fits into the big picture. Disagree with the facts rather than with me as a person. Be patient, persistent, and diplomatic while providing explanations.

Don't Do These Things: Don't refuse to explain details. Don't answer questions vaguely or casually. Don't surprise me.

As a Team Player: I'm conscientious and even tempered. I'm organized. I define the situation, gather and test information. I like to create and maintain systems and enjoy a logical, consistent environment. I pay attention to details and emphasize quality. I'm a good evaluator of the team's progress. I ask important questions and maintain focus on tasks. I offer conservative approaches.

Notes:

Training Instrument 12–16

Problem Solving

PROBLEM SOLVING

Challenge	Potential Solutions

As we discuss our challenges that we "left at the door," make notes of ideas for solutions, as well as other situations for which those solutions might be helpful.

Training Instrument 12–17

Development Plan

Use this form to help you discover the areas in which you excel and what areas you'd like to develop during the coming year. Use this in conjunction with Tool 12–20: Individual Development Plan, to consider your goals and activities as you continue your development.

Name: **Department:**   **Position:**

A. State your understanding of your main duties and responsibilities:

B. What do you feel have been your biggest victories of the past year?

C. What do you feel have been your biggest challenges of the past year?

D. What new skills or knowledge have you gained in the past year that has been helpful to you?

E. What parts of your job do you find most difficult?

F. What parts of your job do you enjoy the most?

G. What parts of your job do you enjoy the least?

H. What do you consider your biggest challenges for the coming year?

I. What could you or your manager do to help you to carry out your main duties and responsibilities?

J. What kind of work would you like to be doing in one / two / five years' time?

continued on next page

Training Instrument 12–17, continued

Development Plan

K. Note areas you would like to learn more about by placing a check in the appropriate column:	I need help and information in this area.	I'm not sure.	I have good skills, but I'd like more development.	My skills are excellent in this area. No help needed.	This doesn't apply to my position.
❏ Business Writing					
❏ Communicating Effectively					
❏ Computer Skills					
❏ Customer Relations / Service					
❏ Decision Making / Problem Solving					
❏ Leadership					
❏ Manager Skills					
❏ Presentation Skills					
❏ Professional Development					
❏ Stress Management					
❏ Teambuilding					
❏ Time Management					
❏ Other Subjects:					

continued on next page

Training Instrument 12–17, continued

Development Plan

L. Based on your victories, achievements, areas of difficulty, and areas of interest, what activities or tasks would you like to focus on during the coming year to help with your continued growth and development?

M. Are there other skills, training, certifications, hobbies, accomplishments, or abilities you have that you would like to able to use in your position? *(For example: Do you have computer skills? Are you skilled at handling difficult customers? Are you good at teaching processes to others?)*

N. Comments, concerns, or other areas you'd like to discuss:

Assessment 12–1

Manager Self-Assessment

1 = Rarely   2 = Infrequently   3 = Sometimes   4 = Often   5 = Most of the Time

As a manager, I . . .

Communication

	1	2	3	4	5
1. Listen more than I talk.	1	2	3	4	5
2. Ask questions to ensure others understand my instructions.	1	2	3	4	5
3. Use positive language in my communications.	1	2	3	4	5
4. Am conscious of my tone and body language when talking.	1	2	3	4	5
5. Ignore all distractions when listening to others.	1	2	3	4	5
6. Practice active listening techniques.	1	2	3	4	5
7. Am seldom misunderstood when I talk to others.	1	2	3	4	5
8. Adjust my communication style to my audience.	1	2	3	4	5
9. Am comfortable giving presentations to groups.	1	2	3	4	5
10. Use a writing style that is professional and seldom misunderstood.	1	2	3	4	5

Customer Service

	1	2	3	4	5
11. Work to ensure that my team is meeting or exceeding customer expectations.	1	2	3	4	5
12. Address and resolve customer complaints quickly.	1	2	3	4	5
13. Ensure staff members understand how their work affects the customer.	1	2	3	4	5
14. Survey customers to find out how we're doing.	1	2	3	4	5
15. Work effectively with internal customers (other departments) to accomplish tasks.	1	2	3	4	5

Performance Management

	1	2	3	4	5
16. Find opportunities to reward and recognize staff.	1	2	3	4	5
17. Set goals with staff members and create action plans.	1	2	3	4	5
18. Conduct formal and informal coaching sessions with staff members.	1	2	3	4	5
19. Regularly observe employee performance to determine potential challenges.	1	2	3	4	5
20. Conduct positive and effective performance evaluations.	1	2	3	4	5

continued on next page

Assessment 12–1, continued

Manager Self-Assessment

Organizational Skills

21. Use a consistent time management system.	1	2	3	4	5
22. Am effective at delegating work.	1	2	3	4	5
23. Know how to use all the technology and tools that are available to me.	1	2	3	4	5
24. Employ a standardized system for project plans.	1	2	3	4	5
25. Can quickly and easily locate any records in my office.	1	2	3	4	5

Professional Development

26. Receive ongoing feedback and coaching on my position.	1	2	3	4	5
27. Know the big picture and my department's role in the organization.	1	2	3	4	5
28. Frequently participate in training and developmental opportunities.	1	2	3	4	5
29. Review my goals and action plans regularly.	1	2	3	4	5
30. Have completed an individual development plan (IDP) in the last year.	1	2	3	4	5

Legal Issues

31. Understand all employment laws.	1	2	3	4	5
32. Know all the steps to handling harassment cases.	1	2	3	4	5
33. Am comfortable with disciplining an employee.	1	2	3	4	5
34. Conduct effective and legal employment interviews.	1	2	3	4	5
35. Document all employee counseling sessions.	1	2	3	4	5

Leadership

36. Monitor my employees' assignments without micromanaging.	1	2	3	4	5
37. Delegate assignments evenly throughout my department.	1	2	3	4	5
38. Follow up on all tasks that I have assigned to staff members.	1	2	3	4	5
39. Solicit input from various resources before making decisions.	1	2	3	4	5
40. Make decisions easily and effectively.	1	2	3	4	5

continued on next page

Assessment 12-1, continued

Manager Self-Assessment

Teamwork

41. Create a positive atmosphere in which teams work together effectively.   1   2   3   4   5

42. Work effectively with persons of diverse personalities and backgrounds.   1   2   3   4   5

43. Regularly solicit input from members of my department.   1   2   3   4   5

44. Ensure that my teams know their purpose and authority level on projects.   1   2   3   4   5

45. Create opportunities for others in my department to take leadership roles.   1   2   3   4   5

Problem Solving

46. Am calm and unbiased when handling office conflicts.   1   2   3   4   5

47. Am able to solve most problems that arise among workers in my department.   1   2   3   4   5

48. Solicit input from those closest to the problem.   1   2   3   4   5

49. Investigate to ensure I'm addressing the real problem, not just a symptom.   1   2   3   4   5

50. Conduct evaluations to review decisions and results.   1   2   3   4   5

Based on the answers above, in which areas are you most effective as a manager?

Which areas could you develop to be a more effective manager?

Assessment 12–2

Evaluation Form

Name (optional): _____   Company: _____

Course: _____   Instructor: _____

Date: _____   Time: _____

Instructions: Answer the questions below. For questions 1 through 10, circle the appropriate number, using the following scale:

1 = Definitely No   2 = No   3 = Not Sure/Not Applicable   4 = Yes   5 = Definitely Yes

1. Did you enjoy this workshop?	1	2	3	4	5
2. Did you obtain the information that you needed?	1	2	3	4	5
3. Will the handouts be valuable as job aids?	1	2	3	4	5
4. Do you feel that the information from this workshop will help improve your management skills?	1	2	3	4	5
5. Would you like to attend an advanced course on this topic?	1	2	3	4	5
6. Did the instructor know the subject matter?	1	2	3	4	5
7. Was the pacing of the class comfortable for you?	1	2	3	4	5
8. Were questions answered completely and clearly?	1	2	3	4	5
9. Did the instructor's presentation style keep your attention and interest in the subject matter?	1	2	3	4	5
10. Would you recommend this program to others?	1	2	3	4	5

11. What would you have liked more of in this program?

12. What would you have liked less of in this program?

13. What is one thing you learned in this program that you will be able to put into practice in the workplace?

Tool 12–1

Coaching Notes

COACHING GUIDE

Employee's Name: **Manager's Name:**

LEARNING OBJECTIVE *What is the area of development for this person? What does he/she need to know how to do more effectively?* 1	**MANAGER'S INVOLVEMENT** *How can manager help in this process? Regular meetings? Progress reports? Allocating time for training?* 4
SUCCESS GUIDELINES *What are the measurable ways to check progress?* 3	**RECOMMENDED RESOURCES** *Are there specific people who can help them learn? Books? Training programs? Online materials? Other?* 2

STEP BY STEP

What the person will do:	What manager will do to support this step:	Deadline:

Tool 12–2

Conflict Management Strategies

CONFLICT MANAGEMENT STRATEGIES

Choose your battles. Determine if this challenge is important enough to warrant intervention.

Set ground rules. Set boundaries to ensure that participants do not resort to personal attacks.

View conflict as an opportunity. Conflict is a sign of differing viewpoints. Those viewpoints keep workplaces from becoming stagnant and losing their creative edge. Remind the parties involved that conflict is an opportunity to look at innovative and unusual solutions.

Schedule a session. Do not jump into conflict management when parties are in a rush, emotional, don't have all the facts, or are under pressure. Schedule the session for a better time.

Do your homework. Get all the facts before beginning a conflict management session.

Meet privately. Follow the adage of "Praise in public, counsel in confidence." Enlist the fewest number of people necessary to reach a solution.

Ask for a preliminary vote. If you are not sure how many people are in disagreement on an issue, take an initial vote to determine the extent of the conflict.

Find areas of agreement. Find areas parties agree on and work from there to determine a solution.

Stick to one issue. If other issues come up during a conflict management session, table them.

Ask questions. Use questions to discover if the challenge is the issue or a symptom of a larger issue.

Listen. Sometimes people just need to vent. Allow them to tell their stories two full times to help remove the emotion and get all the facts. Then direct the discussion toward a solution.

Ask for solutions. Use the formula of "Don't bring a problem without also bringing a potential solution."

Walk in their shoes. Have participants trade sides so that each looks at the issue from the other's point of view.

continued on next page

Tool 12–2, continued

Conflict Management Strategies

List pros and cons. List these publicly so the group can review them.

Review precedents. Review similar situations that were resolved satisfactorily for possible solutions.

Say "I" instead of "you." Instead of "You drive me crazy," try "I feel uncomfortable when you . . . "

Use teamwork language. Use language that removes the concept of one person against another. Put both on the same side against the problem. "What can we do to solve this?"

Collaborate. Define the conflict management session as a problem-solving situation and have all parties work together to solve it.

Brainstorm. Use a creative, no-judging session in which all ideas are thrown in for consideration.

Compromise. Look for what each party will and won't give up and find the middle ground.

Seek alternatives. If one side has a solution and the other side has a differing solution, use those two solutions to create a third alternative solution.

Take a break. When emotions become involved or the conflict escalates, it's a good idea to step away from the discussion and regain perspective.

Enlist an objective negotiator. When all parties have a vested interest in the outcome and have reached an impasse, bring in an outside negotiator to assist in the process.

Assert authority. Sometimes the only answer is to say, "Do it."

Follow up. Ensure that you have follow-up procedures built into your plan so that a challenge doesn't have to be addressed again.

Tool 12–3

Presentation Design Form

Topic

Date	Start Time and End Time	Event / Theme
Attendees	Location	Room Setup

Purpose

Audience Notes

Main Points: The concepts I want to get across to my audience are

1.

2.

3.

continued on next page

Tool 12–3, continued

Presentation Design Form

Opening

Point One

S

E

T

Point Two

S

E

T

Point Three

S

E

T

Review and Restate

continued on next page

Tool 12–3, continued

Presentation Design Form

First Closing

Question-and-Answer Period

Second Closing

Tool 12–4

Agenda Form

AGENDA FORM

Name of Meeting:

Date:	Start and End Times:	Location:

Purpose	By the end of this meeting, we will have . . .

Attendees	Names/Roles:

Time	Agenda Item	Facilitator	Action Items Deadlines Who's Responsible

continued on next page

Tool 12–4, continued

Agenda Form

MEETING COMMUNICATIONS

Name of Meeting:	
Introduction	
Title / Type of Meeting (for example, planning, informational, brainstorming, and so forth) / Date / Start and End Times/ Location	
Purpose	By the end of this meeting, we will have. . .
Why they are being invited . . .	
If they can't attend, they should . . .	
What prework they can do . . .	
How and when they should RSVP . . .	
What they should expect at the meeting . . .	
Other notes . . . (for example, dress code, parking, refreshments, and so forth)	

Tool 12–5

Meeting Planning Form

MEETING PLANNING FORM

Before the Meeting	❑ **Purpose:** What is the subject of this meeting? ❑ **Agenda:** Use agenda form to create detailed schedule ❑ **Invitees:** Name and role of each invitee ❑ **Who Is Needed:** Why are they being invited? What replacement can come if they are not available? ❑ **Confirmations:** Track confirmed attendees ❑ **Outcome Expected:** By the end of this meeting, we will . . . ❑ **Preparation Needed:** What homework can attendees do to be prepared? ❑ **Start and End Times:** Exact times ❑ **Room Setup:** Room layout, materials, audiovisual needs, refreshments
During the Meeting	❑ **Preview Agenda** Supply copies or display publicly (for example, flipchart, Power-Point) ❑ **Assign Duties** Minutes Timekeeper Scribe for flipchart Parliamentarian ❑ **List All Action Items** Specific actions to be taken after this meeting and responsible parties

continued on next page

Tool 12–5, continued

Meeting Planning Form

Closing the Meeting	❏ **Review Action Items from Minutes** Include who, what, when, where, how
Follow Up	❏ **Follow-Up Communication** Confirm when minutes will be distributed ❏ **Next Actions** What is expected of attendees now ❏ **Next Meeting** Date, time, location, and any additional invitees

Facility _____

Contact _____ Title _____

Phone _____ Cell _____

Email _____ Fax _____

Event _____

Day/Date _____ Start Time _____ End Time _____

Location _____ Number of Attendees _____

Notes _____

Room Setup

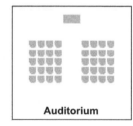

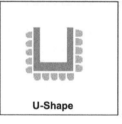

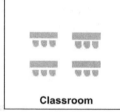

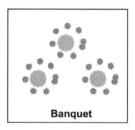

Auditorium   U-Shape   Classroom   Banquet

continued on next page

Tool 12–5, continued

Meeting Planning Form

Create Materials

❏ Agenda
❏ Reference Materials
❏ Written Reports
❏ Sign-In Sheets
❏ Minutes
❏ Audiovisual Materials

❏ Workbooks
❏ Pens
❏ Charts
❏ Exercises
❏ Evaluation Forms
❏ Flipcharts

Test Equipment

❏ TV/VCR
❏ Lights
❏ Overhead
❏ Cassette Player
❏ Easel
❏ Flipchart Pads

❏ Microphone
❏ Laptop/Projector
❏ Slide Projector
❏ Laser Pointer
❏ Screen
❏ Markers

Make Other Arrangements As Needed

❏ Refreshments
❏ Name Badges

Tool 12–6

Minutes Format

AGENDA ITEM	ACTION / OWNER	DISCUSSION NOTES
◆ *Items as listed on meeting agenda*	◆ *Action items, action canceled, in progress, or tabled* ◆ *Person who is responsible for this action item*	◆ *Any background or information that is important to understand this agenda item*

Tool 12–7

Brainstorming

Instructions: Begin your group brainstorming session by writing the topic in a center circle on a flipchart page. List any related topics on the page branching out from the main topic as illustrated below. You can continue to add branches until you have run out of ideas. If the branches also generate additional ideas, continue to branch out from those.

Rules: No judging of ideas. The goal is quantity, not quality. Piggybacking (building on ideas) is allowed. Creativity is encouraged. The wilder the ideas, the better!

Next Steps: Put ideas on a flipchart page. Allow each person in the group to come forward and mark three choices from the ideas. You will choose the items with the most marks as the first ones to try.

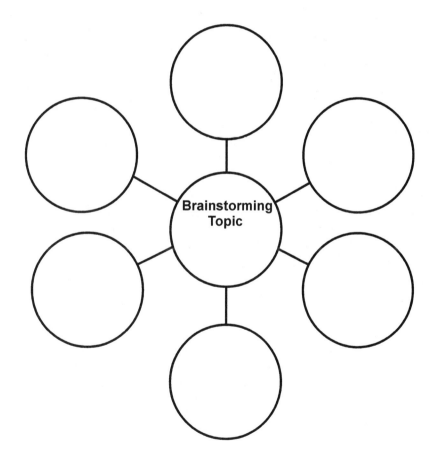

Tool 12–8

Customer Service Formula

CUSTOMER SERVICE FORMULA

Use the following steps to ensure that you reach an acceptable resolution to customer-service challenges.

Listen	The main things a customer wants in a challenging situation are a solution and to know that his or her concerns have been heard.
	Practice active listening skills to ensure you get to the root of the problem. Listen carefully, ask questions, take notes, use appropriate body language and tone, and restate information to ensure that you understand correctly.
Apologize	Apologizing doesn't mean you're accepting blame for a situation. It is simply expressing your regret that a customer is experiencing a negative situation.
Conduct Two-Way Conversation	Ask open-ended questions that can't be answered with a "yes" or "no" so that you can get information on the situation. Summarize and paraphrase what the customer is saying so you can try to get to the root of the problem.
Determine Solution Together	Allow the customer to bring solutions first. Amend his or her solution as needed and see if you can reach an acceptable solution in that manner before moving to alternate solutions.
Explain What Will Happen Next	Give the steps that will happen, deadlines, and any other follow-up actions that you will take to repair the situation.
Thank Them	A sincere thank you at the end of a challenging situation can help restore positive customer opinion. The last thing they hear before they leave should always be a positive comment. Additionally, letting customers know that you appreciate the fact that they called your attention to the problem helps them to feel like a part of the solution.

Tool 12–9

Business Writing Tips

BASIC TIPS FOR BUSINESS WRITING

Write to express, not to impress.	Don't use acronyms (abbreviations) or unfamiliar terms unless you explain them.
Plan your documents.	Consider the audience and what you want them to understand, do, or feel. Use appropriate language for that audience.
Use your subject line.	Subject lines of emails, memos, and letters should be designed to catch the attention of the receiver. In a crowded email inbox, messages can easily be overlooked if you have neglected to include a subject line.
Use active verbs.	Sentences in which the actor is before the action is active voice. (He threw the ball.) Passive voice is when the receiver is first. (The ball was thrown by him.) The active voice is more natural and dynamic.
Use positive language.	Tell what you can do instead of what you can't do. Instead of: We can't deliver that until Thursday. Write: We can deliver that on Thursday. Both lines say the same thing, but the second one keeps a positive tone.
Avoid slang.	This includes emails in which slang might include symbols, initials such as LOL, and all capital letters to indicate shouting.
Summarize your documents.	This includes emails in which slang might include symbols, initials your message with the rule of effective presentations: "Tell them what you're going to tell them, tell them, and tell them what you told them."
Enlist a proofreader.	Especially with major documents, one set of eyes is not enough to review a communication before it is sent out. Ensure that you have a good proofreader review your materials before sending them out.

Tool 12–10

Time Management

PRIORITIZATION OF TASKS

RATE YOUR TASK BY SEEING WHICH OF THESE STATEMENTS DESCRIBES IT.	SCHEDULE YOUR TASKS IN THIS ORDER.
❑ This is urgent. It needs to be done today. ❑ This is important. It will affect my family, my career, or my goals if not done today. ❑ This will lose value if not done today. ❑ This will cause problems or embarrassment if not done today.	**A** Schedule these items first.
❑ Someone else is waiting for this to be completed so they can continue a larger project. ❑ This has a deadline attached to it. ❑ This is not urgent to do today, but it is a part of a goal that is important to me, my family, or my workplace.	**B** Schedule these second. If you do not complete them, move them to the next best day to work on them.
❑ This is not highly important or urgent. ❑ This has no deadline attached to it. ❑ This is an optional activity.	**C** These are optional. You can drop these or move them to another day.

A These items are important and urgent. If you don't do them today, they will lose value or cause problems. These are your high-priority items on your task list. Do them today.

B These items are important, but not urgent. The deadline may be farther off, or they may be developmental tasks that will help you in the long run. If you don't do them today, be sure to reschedule them. If they slip between the cracks, they'll cause problems. As their deadlines approach, they also become more urgent and move into the A category and you won't have a choice on when to do them anymore.

C These are not urgent or important. These are often the items that we keep pushing off to another day. Reconsider whether these need to be done at all. If you have rescheduled them three times, chances are these can be dropped from your list.

Tool 12–11

Project Management

PROJECT MANAGEMENT EXERCISE

For your project, your group will use flipchart pages to

1. Brainstorm the steps of the project.
2. Put the steps in order.
3. Determine how to use the strengths of your group members most effectively.
4. Create a chart showing who is responsible for each step and the deadline.
5. Add any activities for follow up and evaluation of project.
6. Present this plan to the rest of the groups for critique.

A

Your group's project is to present a program on time management for your organization.

The program is to be presented one month from today.

Your team consists of Fred, who knows nothing about time management; Ethel, who is a time-management expert; Lucy, who is excellent at organizing events; and Ricky, who is a wonderful speaker.

B

Your group's project is to present a program on coaching skills for your organization.

This program will be presented in three months.

Your team consists of Ralph, who is not very good at coaching skills; Alice, who is an excellent coach; Trixie, who is organized and methodical; and Norton, who is a great speaker.

C

Your group's project is to present a program on presentation skills for your organization.

This program is to be presented next week.

Your team consists of Gilligan, who has average presentation skills; Professor, who is a expert at writing presentations; Skipper, who is excellent at organizing meetings; and Ginger, who is an accomplished speaker.

Tool 12–12

Decision Grid

PART ONE

1. Determine your overall goals for your department.
2. Brainstorm on the challenges that need to be solved to meet goals.
3. List those challenges in the center column of the Challenges Chart.
4. For each challenge, rate in left column the level of importance or how much impact solving this challenge will have to the organization.
5. For each challenge, rate in the right column the ease or difficulty of solving this challenge.
6. Using these ratings, list your challenges in the Prioritization Chart in Tool 12–13.

CHALLENGES CHART

How important is this to the organization?	Challenges	How hard will this be to solve?
Rating Scale: ☑ High ☑ Medium ☑ Low		Rating Scale: ☑ Easy ☑ Medium ☑ Hard
	A.	
	B.	
	C.	
	D.	
	E.	
	F.	

continued on next page

Tool 12–12

Decision Grid

CHALLENGES CHART

How important is this to the organization?	Challenges	How hard will this be to solve?
Rating Scale: ☑ High ☑ Medium ☑ Low		Rating Scale: ☑ Easy ☑ Medium ☑ Hard
	G.	
	H.	

Next, you'll move on to the Decision Chart and determine priority level.

The next group will present that step.

Tool 12–13

Decision Chart

PART TWO

7. Place each task into the corresponding box by using the level of importance and the difficulty level.
8. The number of the box that the task falls into is the order that it should be addressed to ensure that your first activities are those that are of most importance and greatest ease to complete.
9. Break major challenges into smaller action items and assign tasks to employees, using a project management chart.
10. Follow up by monitoring and reporting accomplishments until task is completed.

PRIORITIZATION CHART

LEVEL OF IMPORTANCE TO ORGANIZATION	DIFFICULTY LEVEL OF SOLVING		
	Easy	Medium	Hard
High	1	2	5
Medium	3	4	7
Low	6	8	9

Tool 12–14

Assessment Chart

Instructions:

1. Determine the attributes that are most important to the position that is being considered. These could include any skills or competencies such as decision making, communication skills, technical knowledge, customer focus, creativity, and so forth.
2. Place the top candidates' names across the top row.
3. Place each skill in the first column.
4. Rank each person on each skill. Each row should have the candidates ranked starting with the top candidate as number 1. The other candidates would be 2, 3, and downward in ranking.
5. Total the numbers for each candidate at the bottom.
6. The candidate with the lowest number is the top candidate.

	Name	Name	Name	Name	Name	Name
Skill A						
Skill B						
Skill C						
Skill D						
Skill E						
TOTAL						

Tool 12–15

Recordkeeping

BASIC NOTES ON RECORDKEEPING

◆ Although the human resources department might have a complete file on each employee, it's important for you to keep your own employee files too.

These files can include

- ◆ job description and revisions

- ◆ résumés

- ◆ performance discussion notes

- ◆ notes on achievements

- ◆ certificates of courses completed

- ◆ compliments from customers, other employees, managers

- ◆ training records

- ◆ communications

- ◆ corrective action goals and deadlines.

◆ Employee records and files should be reviewed before annual performance appraisals to remind you of employee activities throughout the year.

◆ Ensure that employee files are not easily accessible to other employees or visitors.

◆ Check with your human resources department for the specific regulations concerning your employee files. Although there are laws regarding how long many records must be kept, there are also regulations concerning the destruction of past employee files. Get the latest information and review your files to ensure compliance.

continued on next page

Tool 12–15, continued

Recordkeeping

◆ Review your filing systems and discard outdated information every year. Filing systems become overloaded and less useful when valuable information is mixed in with obsolete or unimportant records.

◆ Use the same organization system for your paper files and your computer files. This helps you recall the location of information more easily.

◆ Take time to regularly sort records and paper in your inbox and office. Ask yourself whether you need to

   ◆ act on it

   ◆ delegate it

   ◆ file it

   ◆ toss it.

Tool 12–16

Performance Management Process

Planning Phase

Performance Phase

Review Phase

Tool 12-17

Performance Appraisals

CONDUCTING AN APPRAISAL SESSION

1. Do your homework.

   ♦ Review the employee's files, accomplishments, and challenges.

2. Schedule the session, giving the employee enough time to prepare.

   ♦ If possible, allow the employee to fill out an appraisal form on himself/herself.

   ♦ Ensure that the session is not during a busy production time for the employee.

3. Make the employee comfortable with a private location and provide seating without a desk between you.

4. Start the meeting with a positive comment.

5. Let the employee talk, brag, vent, and so forth.

6. Discuss appraisal ratings with the employee.

   ♦ If he or she filled out a form also, you'll find that the comparison of your ratings is a good basis for discussion of areas where your perspectives differ.

7. Compare documented results with established performance standards.

   ♦ Include specific job performance data to support the ratings given.

   ♦ Summarize any discussions from during the performance period.

   ♦ Keep statements factual and be specific.

   ♦ Focus on behaviors, not attitudes.

   ♦ Let employee know the reason for ratings.

8. Decide together what you can do to solve any challenges.

   ♦ Outline strategies to enhance performance.

   ♦ Agree on mutual SMART (specific, measurable, achievable, relevant, time-bound) goals and objectives.

9. Communicate the performance standards of the next review period.

10. Record the goals so that you both can refer back to them for periodic appraisal.

Tool 12–18

Problem Solving

PROBLEM SOLVING	
STEPS OF PROBLEM SOLVING	NOTES
Define the problem	
Analyze the problem	
Consider alternatives	
Select a solution	
Implement the solution	
Evaluate	

Tool 12–19

Knowledge Management

KNOWLEDGE MANAGEMENT CONCEPTS

TERMS	DEFINITIONS
Career Path	
Competency	
IDP	
Succession Planning	
Explicit Knowledge	
Tacit Knowledge	
Workforce Planning	

Tool 12–20

Individual Development Plan

INDIVIDUAL DEVELOPMENT PLAN (IDP)

Name:	Manager:
Position Title:	Effective Date:

What are my strongest skills?

What skills would I like to develop?

Long-Term Development Goals

ANNUAL ACTION PLAN

Developmental Goal	Steps	Assistance Needed from Manager	Deadline
			Completed
1.			
2.			

continued on next page

Tool 12–20, continued

Individual Development Plan

ANNUAL ACTION PLAN

Developmental Goal	Steps	Assistance Needed from Manager	Deadline / Completed
3.			
4.			

Additional Employee Comments

Employee's Signature: Date:

Manager's Signature: Date:

Using the Website

Go to the website at www.ASTD.org/ManagerSkillsTraining.

DOWNLOADS

Contents of the Website (www.ASTD.org/ManagerSkillsTraining)

The website that accompanies this workbook contains three types of files.

- **Adobe .pdf documents**. These include learning activities, assessments, tools, and training instruments.

- **Microsoft PowerPoint Presentations**. The website includes separate presentations for the one-hour, half-day, one-day, and two-day workshops.

- **Microsoft PowerPoint files of overhead transparency masters.** These files have been formatted to make them more suited for use on overhead transparencies.

Computer Requirements

To read or print the .pdf files on the website, you must have Adobe Acrobat Reader software installed on your system. The program can be downloaded free of charge from the Adobe website, www.adobe.com.

To use or make changes to the contents of the PowerPoint presentation files on the website, you must have Microsoft PowerPoint software installed on your system. If you simply want to view the PowerPoint documents, you must have an appropriate viewer installed on your system. Microsoft provides various viewers free for downloading from its website, www.microsoft.com.

259

Printing From the Website

TEXT FILES

You can print the training materials using Adobe Acrobat Reader. Simply open the .pdf file and print as many copies as you need. The following .pdf documents can be printed directly from the website.

- Learning Activity 11–1: Introductions

- Learning Activity 11–2: The Best Manager I Ever Knew . . .

- Learning Activity 11–3: Interpersonal Skills Practice

- Learning Activity 11–4: Coaching Session Dos and Don'ts

- Learning Activity 11–5: Motivating Employees

- Learning Activity 11–6: Resolving Conflict

- Learning Activity 11–7: Presentation Skills

- Learning Activity 11–8: Effective Meeting Exercise

- Learning Activity 11–9: Customer Service Practice

- Learning Activity 11–10: Business Writing Practice

- Learning Activity 11–11: Q&A Review Session

- Learning Activity 11–12: To Tell the Truth! Review

- Learning Activity 11–13: Time Management Exercise

- Learning Activity 11–14: Project Management Exercise

- Learning Activity 11–15: Decision Charts

- Learning Activity 11–16: Legal Issues

- Learning Activity 11–17: Performance Appraisal Practice

- Learning Activity 11–18: Creating Teams

- Learning Activity 11–19: Problem Solving Activity

- Learning Activity 11–20: Development Plan

- Training Instrument 12–1: The Best Manager I Ever Knew . . .

- Training Instrument 12–2: Interpersonal Skills

- Training Instrument 12–3: Coaching Skills

- Training Instrument 12–4: Motivating Employees

- Training Instrument 12–5: Resolving Conflict

- Training Instrument 12–6: Presentation Skills

- Training Instrument 12–7: Effective Meetings

- Training Instrument 12–8: Customer Service

- Training Instrument 12–9: Business Writing

- Training Instrument 12–10: Time Management

- Training Instrument 12–11: Project Management Chart

- Training Instrument 12–12: Decision Charts

- Training Instrument 12–13: Legal Issues

- Training Instrument 12–14: Performance Appraisals

- Training Instrument 12–15: Creating Teams

- Training Instrument 12–16: Problem Solving

- Training Instrument 12–17: Development Plan

- Assessment 12–1: Manager Self-Assessment

- Assessment 12–2: Evaluation Form

- Tool 12–1: Coaching Notes

- Tool 12–2: Conflict Management Strategies

- Tool 12–3: Presentation Design Form

- Tool 12–4: Agenda Form

- Tool 12–5: Meeting Planning Form

- Tool 12–6: Minutes Format

- Tool 12–7: Brainstorming

- Tool 12–8: Customer Service Formula

- Tool 12–9: Business Writing Tips

- ◆ Tool 12–10: Time Management

- ◆ Tool 12–11: Project Management

- ◆ Tool 12–12: Decision Grid

- ◆ Tool 12–13: Decision Chart

- ◆ Tool 12–14: Assessment Chart

- ◆ Tool 12–15: Recordkeeping

- ◆ Tool 12–16: Performance Management Process

- ◆ Tool 12–17: Performance Appraisals

- ◆ Tool 12–18: Problem Solving

- ◆ Tool 12–19: Knowledge Management

- ◆ Tool 12–20: Individual Development Plan

POWERPOINT SLIDES

You can print the presentation slides directly from the website using Microsoft PowerPoint. Simply open the .ppt files and print as many copies as you need. You can also make handouts of the presentations by printing three "slides" per page. These slides will be in color, with design elements embedded. PowerPoint also permits you to print these in grayscale or black-and-white, although printing from the overhead masters file will yield better black-and-white representations. Many trainers who use personal computers to project their presentations bring along viewgraphs just in case there are glitches in the system. The overhead masters can be printed form the PowerPoint .pps files.

Adapting the PowerPoint Slides

You can modify or otherwise customize the slides by opening and editing them in the appropriate application. However, you must retain the denotation of the original source of the material—it is illegal to pass it off as your own work. You may indicate that a document was adapted from this workbook, written by Christee Atwood, and copyrighted by ASTD. The files will open as "Read Only," so before you adapt them you will need to save them onto your hard drive under a different file name.

Showing the PowerPoint Presentations

On the website, the following PowerPoint presentations are included:

- ◆ One-Hour.ppt

- ◆ Half-Day.ppt

- ◆ Full-Day. ppt

- ◆ Two-Day.ppt

Having the presentations in a .ppt format means that they automatically show full screen when you double-click on a file name. You also can open Microsoft PowerPoint and launch the presentation from there.

Use the space bar, the enter key, or mouse clicks to advance through a show. Press the backspace key to back up. Use the escape key to abort a presentation. If you want to blank the screen to black while the group discusses a point, press the B key. Pressing it again restores the show. If you want to blank the screen to a white background, do the same with the W key. See Table A-1 for tips on using PowerPoint.

We strongly recommend that trainers practice making presentation with the PowerPoint slides before using them in live training situations. You should be confident that you can cogently expand on the points featured in the presentations and discuss the methods for working through them. If you want to engage your training participants fully (rather than worrying about how to show the next slide), become familiar with this simple technology before you need to use it. A good practice is to insert notes into the Speaker's Notes feature of the PowerPoint program, print them out, and have them in front of you when you present the slides.

Table A–1   Navigating Through a PowerPoint Presentation

KEY	POWERPOINT "SHOW" ACTION
Space bar *or* Enter *or* Mouse click	Advance through custom animations embedded in the presentation
Backspace	Back up to the last projected element of the presentation
Escape	Abort the presentation
B *or* b B *or* b *(repeat)*	Blank the screen to black Resume the presentation
W *or* w W *or* w *(repeat)*	Blank the screen to white Resume the presentation

Printed Materials

Alpha Editors. *Every Manager's Desk Reference*. Indianapolis, IN: Pearson Education, 2002.

Bacal, Robert. *Performance Management*. New York: McGraw-Hill, 1999.

Buckingham, Marcus. *First, Break All The Rules*. New York: Simon & Schuster, 1999.

Buhler, Patricia. *Streetwise Human Resources Management*. Avon, MA: Adams Media, 2002.

Caroselli, Marlene. *Leadership Skills for Managers*. New York: McGraw-Hill. 2000.

Center for Creative Leadership. *Handbook of Leadership Development*. San Francisco: Jossey-Bass, 1998.

Charney, Cyril. *The Instant Manager*. New York: AMACOM, 2004.

Covey, Stephen. *Seven Habits of Highly Effective People*. New York: Simon and Schuster, 1989.

Fisher, Sharon G. *The Manager's Pocket Guide to Performance Management*. Amherst, MA: HRD Press, 1997.

Franklin Covey Style Guide for Business and Technical Communication. Salt Lake City, UT: Franklin Covey Company, 1997.

Gebelein, Susan H., Lisa A. Stevens, Carole J. Skube, David G. Lee, Brian L. Davis, and Lowell W. Hellervik. *Successful Manager's Handbook: Development Suggestions for Today's Managers*. Minneapolis, MN: Personnel Decisions International, 2001.

Goleman, Daniel. *Emotional Intelligence*. New York: Bantam Books, 1995.

James, John, and Dan Baldwin. *Restaurant Management*. Avon, MA: Adams Media Corporation, 2003.

Kerzner, Harold D. *Project Management*. New York: Wiley, 2001.

Littauer, Florence. *Personality Plus*. Grand Rapids, MI: Fleming H. Revell, a division of Baker Book House Company, 1992.

MacKenzie, Gordon. *Orbiting the Giant Hairball: A Corporate Fool's Guide to Surviving with Grace.* New York: Penguin Putnam, 1996.

Maslow, Abraham H. *Motivation and Personality* (2nd ed.). New York: Harper and Row, 1970.

McNally, David. *Even Eagles Need a Push.* New York: Dell, 1990.

Merson, Len. *The Instant Productivity Toolkit.* Naperville, IL: Sourcebooks, 2005.

Nakone, Lanna. *Organizing for Your Brain Type: Finding Your Own Solution to Managing Time, Paper, and Stuff.* New York: St. Martin's Griffin, 2005.

National Restaurant Association Educational Foundation. *Human Resources Management and Supervision.* Upper Saddle River, NJ: National Restaurant Association Educational Foundation, 2007.

Nelson, Bob. *Managing for Dummies.* Foster City, CA: IDG Books, 1996.

Newstrom, John, and Edward Scannell. *The Big Book of Teambuilding Games.* New York: McGraw-Hill, 1998.

Orey, Maureen, and Jenni Prisk. *Communications Skills Training.* Alexandria, VA: ASTD Press, 2004.

Pearson, Judy C., Paul E. Nelson, Scott Titsworth, and Lynn Harter. *Human Communication.* New York: McGraw-Hill, 2003.

Ritchey, Tom, and Alan Axelrod. *I'm Stuck, You're Stuck: Breakthrough to Better Work Relationships and Results by Discovering Your DiSC Behavioral Style.* San Francisco, CA: Berrett-Koehler Publishers, 2002.

Smith, Jim Jr. *Crash and Learn.* Alexandria, VA: ASTD Press, 2006.

Smith, Perry M. *Rules & Tools for Leaders: A Down-to-Earth Guide to Effective Managing.* New York: Avery Publishing Group, 1998.

Stettner, Morey. *Skills for New Managers.* New York: McGraw-Hill, 2000.

Straub, John. *The Rookie Manager: A Guide to Surviving Your First Year in Management.* New York: AMACOM, 1999.

Straw, Julie, and Alison Brown Cerier. *The 4-Dimensional Manager: DISC Strategies for Managing.* San Francisco, CA: Berrett-Koehler Publishers, 2002.

Streibel, Barbara J. *The Manager's Guide to Effective Meetings.* New York: McGraw-Hill, 2003.

Weiss, Alan. *The Unofficial Guide to Power Managing.* Foster City, CA: IDG Books Worldwide, 2000.

◆

Christee Gabour Atwood is a speaker, trainer, and knowledge management adviser who specializes in helping companies share the knowledge in their organizations. She has worked with corporations, associations, *Fortune* 500 companies, and governmental entities in analyzing, developing, and presenting programs to develop communication and leadership skills. Recipient of the 2006 Outstanding Adjunct Faculty Award at Baton Rouge Community College, Atwood's background includes radio personality, television host and anchor, and newspaper and magazine columnist. She also has served as executive director for state associations, editor/publisher of various trade and professional magazines, and CEO of The Communications Workshop. Atwood is a master facilitator for the Small Business Training Center in Baton Rouge, Louisiana, and has received training certifications from various organizations, including Franklin Covey and AchieveGlobal. And, because she believes humor is a vital part of effective communications, she also teaches "But UnSeriously Folks!"—a course on the effective use of humor in the workplace, which is based on her experiences in stand-up comedy. Her other books include *Succession Planning Basics* (ASTD Press 2007) and *Three Feet Under: Journal of a Midlife Crisis,* which is a humorous look at the episodes of midlife. *Manager Skills Training* is Atwood's third book with ASTD Press. Her other current ASTD Press title is *Succession Planning* (2007) and *Presentation Skills Training* (2008). She can be reached at Christee@Christee.biz or by visiting SuccessionPlanningBasics.blogspot.com.